Thawing Childhood Abandonment Issues

www.Internet-of-the-Mind.com
Email: dcarter73@msn.com
Phone: (573) 634-2254

Or Write to:
Don Carter, MSW, LCSW
83 South Larand Dr.
Lake MyKee
Holts Summit, MO 65043

TABLE OF CONTENTS

Releasing Blocked Emotions
Closure Exercise
AUDIOS: *Spiritual Release & Reimprint this Stage*

Chapter 1

"What the hell is wrong with you?"

Comedian Bill Cosby has often observed that one of a child's most frequent answers to questions posed by their parents is "I don't know." He forgets to mention that one of a parent's most frequent questions to their children is some variation of *"What the hell is wrong with you?"* I always hated that question. How was I supposed to answer it? ... *"Well, Dad, I'm very happy you asked because I think we really need to talk about this. You see, my childhood dependency needs have not been getting met lately and, as a result, I am suffering from a pretty bad case of low self-esteem and some abandonment issues. If you could see your way clear to lighten up on me a bit I might have a chance to get back on track."* I doubt that would have gone over very well.

I am not sure that my alternative approach was much better for my own kids. I modified the question into a little game. When I found myself wanting to ask one of them, *"What the hell is wrong with you?"* I would stop, raise an eyebrow just a bit, look at them for a moment, and then curiously inquire, *"What grade are you in?"* They would give the answer to which I would smile and say, *"Oh ... that explains it! Maybe they don't teach you about this until next year."*

Motivation

Motivation has been defined as a drive, a need, a desire to do something. In human beings, motivation involves both conscious and unconscious drives. It is this writer's belief that people all have one *ultimate* motive in common. This motive drives everything we think, everything we feel, and everything we do from the time we wake in the morning until we go to sleep at night. I believe this motive is simply to be happy.

In this case, the term *happiness* does not necessarily refer to a feeling or emotion. Feelings come and go so it is not realistic (nor desirable) to hope to stay in one emotional state. Rather, used in this context, happiness is more like a universal *state of being* that describes and contains other states of being such as: contentment, satisfaction, fulfillment, completeness, and wholeness. Again, it is this *pursuit of happiness that is at the root of everything we think, everything we feel, and everything we do.* We all have this same ultimate goal in common, and we are all doing the best we can with what we have to get as close to that ideal as possible. If all of our efforts fail, and we move too far away from the ideal then things can go very wrong, as in the case of someone who can feel empty, unhappy, and unmotivated.

As our ultimate goal in life, the desire to be happy motivates us to make decisions based upon what will move us closer to the positive end of a continuum. On the negative end of this continuum is pain, something we try very hard to stay away from. Most of us do not like pain, but it does have a very important role in our lives. Pain is a warning system that tells us when we are moving in the wrong direction, taking us further away from our ultimate goal.

Granted, we sometimes purposefully make decisions that we know are going to hurt, in the short-term anyway. However, even these painful decisions are driven by the desire to be happy because we know that in the long run we will gain from the short-term pain. For example, deciding not to marry the person of our dreams until we finish college and get our finances in order may be painful in the short-term but very rewarding in the long run. It may even play a part in whether the marriage succeeds or fails. When we make decisions like this, we are said to be mature because we can delay gratification.

There are other times we make decisions that don't make us happy such as when we act without hesitating long enough to think it through. For example, impulsively taking out a new line of credit or buying a new car when we cannot afford it may provide some instant gratification but soon leads to buyer's remorse and other negative long-term consequences when the bills start coming in. Buyer's remorse is an example of an emotional consequence we suffer when we realize what we have done and how it is going to lead to our future unhappiness. When we don't stop and think it through before we act, we are said to have impulse control problems, a sign of immaturity.

When immaturity persists into adulthood it suggests that some sort of developmental delay has taken place such as emotional arrest. Developmental delays are usually the consequence of unmet childhood needs. Frozen feeling-states are another way of describing these developmental issues. We will explore these concepts in great detail throughout this book. We will also explore a very simple, yet incredibly powerful formula, A → B (→ = leads to). This formula is where A is a choice we make and B is the outcome. The outcome is where we find ourselves on the pleasure and pain continuum as a consequence of our choice.

Maslow's Hierarchy

The American psychologist Abraham Maslow (1968) devised a six-level hierarchy of needs that, according to his theory, drive human behavior. I believe that each of these needs must be met in order for one to truly be happy. Maslow progressively ranks human needs as follows:

1. Physiological - food, shelter, clothing;
2. Security and safety;
3. Love and feelings of belonging;
4. Competence, prestige, and esteem;
5. Curiosity and the need to know; and
6. Self-Actualization

Maslow suggests that each preceding need must be met, at least to some degree, before one can go on to the next level. For instance, a child may not be able to pay attention in class if she is preoccupied with hunger. Maslow refers to the first four levels as deficiency needs and the last two growth needs.

While these needs are important for all human beings, special attention must be given to how we meet these needs in children because, as we shall see, it is the meeting of these needs, or not meeting them, that sets in motion a whole series of events that have an impact on the adjustment of that child. In children, deficiency needs are also referred to as dependency needs because children cannot meet these needs themselves; they *depend* upon their caretakers to meet these needs for them.

Childhood Dependency Needs

Small children cannot meet their own needs, much like a plant cannot water itself. As we grow, we become more *independent* and able to meet more and more of our needs on our own. There are two groups of dependency needs. The first group is the survival needs. These are what Maslow calls the basic needs for food, shelter, clothing, medical attention, safety and protection. If these needs are not met, at least to a minimal degree, the child is likely to die. Notice that the survival needs include the child's need to feel safe and protected. If a child does not feel safe she cannot relax. She is always on guard, scanning her environment for danger. Her anxiety level is very high, and she has to stay alert and "tuned in" to everything going on around her causing her to become hyper-vigilant, hyper-alert, and/or hyper-sensitive. Feeling safe helps children relax; if they can't relax they can't play. If they can't play it interferes with their growth. Play is how children learn and grow along normal developmental lines.

Because feeling safe is so important, children have a built-in psychological defense mechanism called idealization which functions to help them feel safe. This is necessary for them to be able to relax enough to play which, again, is the business of being a child. Through idealization, children (not referring to teenagers here) set their parents up on a pedestal, seeing them as godlike creatures. This makes them feel safe because "if I am protected by a godlike creature and then nothing can get to me" (Bradshaw). Of course children cannot yet think that way, but they "get it" that way in an emotional sense. We will come back to idealization later.

The emotional dependency needs are what Maslow refers to as the basic needs for love and esteem. These are the needs that nourish a child emotionally. If they get these needs met fully on a consistent basis, children thrive and flourish. If they don't get these needs met, they suffer to an extent proportional to their lack of need fulfillment. John Bradshaw (1992, 2005) refers to the following as primary emotional dependency needs: *Time*, *Attention*, *Affection*, and *Direction*.

Time = Love

Bradshaw and others point out that a small child equates time with love. In his video *Shame and Addiction*, Bradshaw states, "Little kids get it that whatever their parents give their time to is what they love." So if dad is gone working ten to twelve hours a day, which may be his way of showing love, the kids feel that dad loves what he is doing more than he loves them. They don't understand about budgets and bills. They don't understand that this may be dad's way of demonstrating his love for the family. All they know is he is usually gone and when he comes home, he is too tired to spend time with them. All he wants to do is rest, read the paper, and watch some TV. The main point here is that the children need time from *both* parents, not just one. They need enough time from each parent to get the message that they are loved as much as anyone else in the family. It is not as much of a question of quantity as it is of consistency and quality. "Quality time" is when the child's other three emotional needs are also being met.

Attention = Worth

Just as children equate time with love, they get it that attention equals worth or value. Attention is more than just listening to the children; it is *attending* to them. Parents attend to children when they take them seriously, show genuine concern and curiosity about who they are, what they think, how they feel. Attentive parents notice when the child is struggling with a feeling and help figure out what it is and what to do about it. They are engaged in their child's life, to the extent that they know how their child's day went, who the child is hanging out with, what the highlight of the week was, etc.

Children need lots of attention, and if they don't get it their behavior becomes attention-seeking. This is not deliberate on their part. Most of the time, children really don't know why they act-out in ways that are obviously designed to get attention. They are compelled to do it because they *need* attention, not because they *want* attention. When was the last time you heard this statement, "Oh, he's trying to get attention, just ignore him." Sometimes this is bad advice, other times it is not. There are two reasons kids show attention-seeking behavior: when they are not getting enough attention, and when they have been used to getting too much attention. The latter will be discussed when we look at the need for direction.

Affection = Approval

As a therapist, it has been my experience that affection is the area where many families seem to fall short. Many of my clients have told me, "Well, mine were not the most affectionate parents in the world, but I always knew they loved me." I am sure it is true that they were loved. However, I am also aware that kids need hugs, kisses, pats on the back, and words of encouragement on a regular basis. Displays of affection are how approval messages are sent from the parent to the child. Affection says "I like you," "I like who you are and who you are becoming," "I am glad you are my child," I am happy I get to be your parent," "I am grateful we have been blessed with you." In other words, affection is how children get the message that they are approved of by the parent. How many of us know a child who is not sure what his father thinks of him? Or one who is uncertain whether she measures up to her mother's expectations? How many are sure that we *don't* measure up?

Kids who don't get enough affection display approval-seeking behaviors such as people-pleasing. They act-out their need for approval by trying to please mom or dad. When their attempts go un-noticed they try harder and harder to please them, setting in motion the development of an ingrained pattern of people-pleasing behavior. We will look more at these types of behavioral patterns later.

Direction:

Guidance = Competence

Children are born not knowing how to do things. They are biologically programmed to survive in the wild, but everything about how to live in our culture must be learned, including relationships. Our caretakers are our teachers. Dad shows us how to be a man in the world; Mom shows us how to be a woman in the world; and they both show us how men and women get along with each other. In other words, our cultural and interpersonal programming is not biologically endowed but comes through the modeling of our parents, whether they realize it or not.

In the ideal situation, parents do realize the powerful influence their behavior has on the development of their children. They also know that to be good teachers they have to be available and approachable: i.e., the children know when and where to find dad or mom, and they know that it is okay to go to them for advice and assistance. To be available goes back to the issues of time and attention, parents must make the time to attend to the questions of their kids. To be approachable they must also be patient, tolerant, and affectionate. Good teachers understand that kids need repetition to learn. They may have to ask and be shown more than once in order to develop competence at a certain task.

A sense of competence and mastery are critical to the development of a child's sense of self. For instance, when parents teach a child to ride a bike, they hold on and hold on until the child gets her balance, and then they let go. Usually, the child will crash a time or two, but soon she takes off and rides. Did you ever see children who take off on a bike for the first time? They light up like a Christmas tree and almost universally shout the same thing: *"Look at me! I'm doing it!"* This is a statement of competence and provides a huge boost to their ego. After a while, you might hear the same child shout, *"Look at me! I'm doing it with no hands!"* This shows that the child now has a sense of mastery. Do you ever wonder why kids do the same thing repeatedly once they become proficient at it and avoid things they might not do well? Satisfying the need for a sense of competence and mastery is the reason. Children need as many I-can-do-it experiences as we can give them. Things like tying their shoe for the first time, driving a car, going on a date, learning to dance, getting good grades, learning to cook, hitting a baseball, etc.

Parents help their kids get the I-can-do-it experience by helping them develop the skill sets necessary to perform a given task. This again requires time, attention, and affection. If children learn the fundamentals of something, they are much more likely to succeed. If they try to learn on their own, without any ideas of the fundamentals, they are likely to fail more times than they need to. Kids who fail too much eventually give up trying. They need available and approachable teachers to help them learn.

Approachable teachers help without resorting to criticism when working with a child. It is truly an art, and most of us were raised on criticism so it is difficult to learn. Healthy critical feedback comes with love, tolerance, and without shame. For example, helpful criticism might sound like this: "I know it's difficult." "You are doing very well …I fell off more than this when I was your age." "I know you can do it, let's try one more time for today." Shameful criticism sounds like this: "Oh come on, don't be a big baby!" "You always make things harder than they should be." "Your brother took off on his first try … are you going let him make you look bad?"

One other issue regarding guidance is *over-protection,* which must also be explored here. There are some families that have rigid, sometimes extremely over-controlling rules designed to "protect" the child. For example, "The training wheels don't come off until you are twelve years old," "You cannot climb trees," "You can go outside but don't do anything," and "You must wear a football helmet if you are going to get on the swing set." They also do everything for the child, even that which children should be able to do themselves. Over-protection and over-involvement is a result of a parent's inability to tolerate any chance that their child might get hurt, physically or emotionally (failure). This can easily be mistaken for love, when, in fact, it is not. This is more about the parent's need to feel safer than it is about the child's need for protection. The child not only misses out on the I-can-do-it experiences but also gets a message from the god-like creatures in his life that *he can't do it*–a feeling of incompetence is the result. The child feels *"If Mom and Dad don't think I can do it, then I must not be able to do it."* These kids usually end up with all kinds of problems with indecision, shame, fear, and anxiety.

Discipline = Character

Discipline is the second form of direction kids need. Children are born without the internal structures to control their own impulses. Therefore, they were given external structures, called parents, to help them. When parents set limits for their children they are telling them "Here's the line, if you step over it this is what happens" (A → B). Setting and enforcing good limits helps develop the internal structures necessary for children to control their own impulses. These structures build character. Character consists of two primary internal structures: *values*–the knowledge of right and wrong, and *self-discipline*–the ability to delay or deny the gratification of impulses based upon that knowledge.

If we remember a simple formula, A → B, then we will have quite a bit of knowledge about setting good limits. Cause-and-effect seems to be a law of the universe. Simply put, when our *behavior* (A) is a good thing, then the *outcome* (B) should also a good thing; when A is a bad thing, then B should also a bad thing. The consequences we receive (positive or negative) shape our behaviors by reinforcing the good and dissuading the bad. While this formula is simple in theory, it is difficult in practice because this life does not always go as it "should," as we shall see in the next chapter.

Healthy limits are firm, effective, and consistent. The limits (B) are also connected and proportionate to the behavior (A);

i.e., let the punishment fit the crime. When parents set and consistently enforce good limits for their children, they are teaching an important law of the universe. This will be extremely significant to children later in their adulthood when life becomes their teacher. Conversely, when we are inconsistent with the limits, or they are inappropriate for the behavior, then we are doing our children a huge disservice. For instance, when a teenager does "A" (e.g., comes home smelling of alcohol), and they should receive "B" (e.g., grounded for a certain period of time) but the parent feels sorry for them because the prom is this weekend, so they provide "C" (Letting them off the hook and giving them $50 to have a good time) then the message sent and received is A → C, In other words, "If I screw up when it really counts, Mom and Dad will bail me out." Providing "C" when "B" should follow interferes with the grand design, *enabling* problem behaviors to persist.

Decisions about good limits are not always easy. Some limits must be nonnegotiable, e.g. those related to the safety of the child and those connected with strongly held family values, while others can be structured to teach the child flexibility and how to compromise. For example, when the child does "A" (breaks curfew by thirty minutes *for the first time ever*), and the agreed upon consequence is "B" (grounded for the next two weekends) the negotiated agreement might be that the child can choose which two weekends of the next month to be grounded.

Another word for limits is boundaries. When parents set and consistently enforce healthy limits, they are helping their child learn healthy boundaries. Children who don't know where the boundaries are tend to feel unsafe. Spoiled-child syndrome is what results when a child is given blanket approval for everything he or she does. When there are little or no consequences provided for these children, they push the limits and push the limits until someone steps in to say "no!" Misbehavior in this case is *discipline-seeking* behavior. The child is unconsciously acting-out his *need* for help with controlling his impulses, and they are compelled to get it. Just as in over-protection, the well-meaning intentions of the over-indulgent parent backfire. Usually, the parents are trying very hard not to hurt the child's self-esteem with criticism, so they rarely provide this form of protection. The child gets the message that the god-like creatures in his life have no expectations of him because they are not capable of living up to any expectations due to incompetence.

Other forms of discipline include the ones that moms and dads model for us in their own daily behavior, including good manners, hygiene, work ethics, etc. We watch and learn from them. The old adage *"Do as I say, not as I do"* is not very effective in helping our kids develop and internalize these daily disciplines. The most effective tool in teaching kids is good role-modeling. Limits and consequences simply reinforce what we demonstrate.

The Iceberg Model

Throughout the book, I will refer to *the Iceberg Model* [Fig.1] to develop a picture or roadmap of what happens when childhood dependency needs go unmet. The Iceberg Model has been used as a visual tool to simplify very abstract concepts of being human by many people, including Sigmund Freud, Friel and Friel, and Dr. Larry Crabb, to name a few. You will hear many of the ideas and principles of the pioneers in the field of addiction theory such as Charles Whitfield MD, John Bradshaw, Pia Mellody, Vernon Johnson, Claudia Black, Terrence Gorski, and many others. They have been my teachers on such topics as addiction, codependency, Adult/Child Syndrome, abandonment, shame, and childhood dependency needs. I have used the Iceberg to integrate some of their ideas, along with many of my own, into this unified model of the issues underlying most addictive, mental, emotional, interpersonal, and even spiritual problems. To delve deeper into many of the concepts presented here see Appendix A for a list of suggested readings.

It has been my experience that most people have a profound revelation about who they are, where they came from, and where they can go from here after hearing the Iceberg lecture. It is my hope that this book will produce the same results for you, the reader. Again, the best thing about this model is that it keeps some very abstract ideas relatively simple and provides a concrete roadmap for understanding and preparing for change. So let's get started ...

Figure 1: Iceberg Model

The Iceberg represents a human being. The waterline represents the dividing line between what is in our consciousness or awareness (above) and what is in our unconsciousness or our unawareness (below). The deeper one looks beneath the surface symbolizes the deeper we are into our unawareness or our unconscious. It is my hope readers will have a better idea of how to achieve that one "ultimate motive," which we all have in common by the time they have finished reading.

Please, if you are a parent, as you read, try to focus on at least as much of your own childhood experience as you do on the experience of your children. This book is not about blaming parents because, as we shall discuss later, the vast majority of parents do the best they can with what they are given. If you are reading this book, chances are that sometime in the past you have said something like, *"My kids are going to have it better than I did!"* This statement is an affirmation that you understand what it is like not to get your dependency needs met, at least to some degree.

Chapter 2

Anatomy of an Emotional Wound

According to Linn, Fabricant, and Linn (1988), in the early 1900s if you were born into an orphanage in the United States you were likely to be dead by the time you were two years old. This was according to a study done by Dr. Henry Chapin, a pediatrician in New York City. There was another pediatrician, Dr. Fritz Talbot, who found those statistics unacceptable. He discovered an orphanage in Dusseldorf, Germany where the mortality rate was the same as the general population, so he went to investigate. The doctor found that the orphanage followed very similar policies and procedures as those here in America with one small difference. There was an older woman named Anna, who carried a child on each hip. The director of the orphanage told Dr. Talbot, "When we have done everything medically possible for a baby, and it is still not doing well, we turn the child over to old Anna. Whenever a child cried the woman would pick the child up, hold him or her, and give motherly love. A few minutes with old Anna literally meant the difference between life and death for some kids."

When this doctor came back to the United States, he shared his findings and several institutions recruited volunteers to do the same things Anna did. Not surprisingly in a very short time the mortality rate quickly became consistent with the general population.

Abandonment

Children who get their dependency needs met fully on a regular basis will thrive, flourish, and grow at a healthy pace. Life will be good for these kids. In the worst-case scenario, kids who do not get their needs met at all will experience a failure to thrive, and many will die. Let us use the analogy of an emotional gas tank; if our needs are met fully we feel full, complete, satisfied, content, and happy. If we don't get our needs met at all we feel a great emptiness inside. I have heard this emptiness described in many ways: a black hole, a void, a vacuum, an ache, or a longing. Perhaps we get our needs met half-way; we feel half-full but something is missing, and we still feel an ache. These are emotional wounds, also known as *original pain*, and they result from an *abandonment* of our childhood dependency needs.

A Word about Blame

When parents do not meet the needs of their children, it is not usually because the parents don't love them. I say "usually" because there are those cases that one cannot understand, accept, explain, or excuse for any reason. However, most parents do the best they can, given the internal and external resources they possess, to take care of their children. In fact, I cannot count the times I have heard parents say, "I try hard to make sure my kids have it better than I did." This speaks very loudly to me. It says that these parents are familiar with unmet dependency needs. So, most often, it is not the parent's lack of love or effort that is to blame. It is usually because of one of the following reasons that abandonment occurs:

1. Circumstances: For example, if one parent dies and the other must take two jobs to care for ten children, circumstances are to blame for this, not the parents. None-the-less the children get hurt in the process.

2. Wounded people wound people: Parents cannot demonstrate much more than they have been given. Our parents were raised by their parents who likely were also wounded, and they were raised by their parents, etc. Maybe dad is an alcoholic; he has a disease that impaired his ability function in his major life roles, including his ability to be the kind of father his kids need him to be. He did not aspire to become alcoholic. Alcoholism chooses you, you don't choose it. Perhaps mom is so chronically depressed she can't leave a dark room much less take care of anyone else; she didn't

choose that. However, the primary issue for parents is that they are wounded themselves, sometimes moderately, other times severely because their parents were also wounded, and their parents were wounded, etc. Whatever the issue, the result is wounded children.

Again, it is not usually a question of whether our parents loved us, or even if they did the best they could for us. Many people get stuck on this truth and end up saying, "So why go back and dig all that up? They did the best they could and that is that. You can't change the past." To those people, I say keep reading, this book will show you why it is important to "dig all that up." Suffice it to say here that assigning blame is *not* the reason.

Children have not yet developed the skills to cope effectively with emotional pain. It seems they can handle a broken arm better than a broken heart. They rely heavily on a defense mechanism called repression to push the emotional wound deep into their unawareness [Fig. 2]. They also act-out their pain in various ways as a survival instinct which calls attention to it so the adults in their life can assess, diagnose, and respond to them. If the adults are unresponsive, and the child continues to experience abandonment the wounds accumulate.

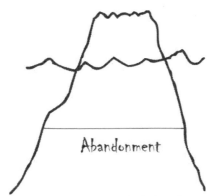

Abandonment

Figure 2: The wound of abandonment

The extent of the wounds may be mild, moderate, or severe depending upon the extent of the abandonment. Mild to moderate cases of wounding comes from situations in which the child does not fully or consistently get their emotional dependency needs met. There may be few overt signs of family dysfunction or abuse. For instance, it may be that one or both parents are able to give reasonable amounts time, attention and direction but are unable to express affection. The words *"I love you"* may rarely be heard, if at all, in this family. A lack of hugs, kisses, and other forms of emotional warmth leave a child to wonder how they measure up in the eyes of their parents. It makes matters even worse when the child lives in a shame-based family system. In such families the children get messages of disapproval through constant criticism rather than messages of approval and warmth.

A shame-based family system is characterized by the parent's use of shame to provide direction to the child. For instance, when a five-year-old child scrapes his knee the parent, or parents, might tell the child to stop crying because *"Big boys don't cry."* They may also simply ignore the child until he or she stops crying. Similarly, when the child makes a mistake the parent might say, *"What's wrong with you?"* or *"Why can't you be more like your sister?"*

Sometimes the shaming goes to extremes, especially when a wounded, shame-based parent is angry: *"You are going to end up in prison!" "You'll never amount to anything!" "You never were any good; why do you do this to me?"* These comments are often accompanied by slaps or even punches from the parent. In shame-based families these types of comments and behaviors are often intended to "help" the child learn right from wrong. However, while the intended "help" may actually produce the intended result the next time, another result is emotional wounds for the child. Shame is discussed in more detail in the next section of this chapter.

Another common abandonment scenario occurs when one of the parents is physically absent much of the time. The parent may be a "workaholic" who cannot seem to stop working long enough to find time for his family. The workaholic rationalizes his absence and breaks promises to be there for the child in the same way an alcoholic rationalizes her drinking and breaks promises to stop or control it better.

By now, the reader may begin to suspect that abandonment and wounding must happen on some level to most, if not all, of us. I believe it is true that all of us experience emotional wounds in life, but *not all of us* experience abandonment. The best example is when we lose someone or something important to us. Grief is a natural part of living, and one cannot escape an encounter with it for long in this world. When someone or something becomes important to us, we bond with it on an emotional level. Emotional wounds result when this bond is breaking or broken. Grief is the process we must go through to let go of the attachment and heal from the resulting loss-related emotional wound.

The absence of a parent may be perfectly justifiable as when a military parent is abruptly deployed overseas for a year or longer. As already mentioned, little kids get it that parents love what they give their time to. So if the child gets little or no time from a parent, the child tends to *experience it* as little or no love, regardless of the reason for the absence. Whether or not it results in abandonment in the case of circumstantial, unavoidable, or justifiable absences, such as the above example of deployment, is determined by what happens before, during, and after the absence of the parent.

There has been much written that suggests the terms "abandonment" and "loss" are interchangeable. While both result in emotional wounds, the author believes they are not interchangeable terms and that an important distinction must be made. *Abandonment always involves loss for the child, but loss does not always involve abandonment.* Loss-related wounds can heal if the person possesses the psychological support and emotional coping skills necessary to aid in the grieving process. Children who have emotionally healthy, responsive parents tend to get their needs met consistently. Because of that, they are equipped either internally with their own coping skills (depending on their age) and/or externally with parents who are able to provide the necessary support through the grief process.

When children cannot put into words what they are experiencing, whether it be from abandonment or other significant losses, their pain must find expression somehow and does so through *compulsive* patterns of behavior commonly referred to as "acting-out." When their needs are going unmet, children are *compelled by instinct* to act-out their needs through behaviors designed to elicit an appropriate response from caregivers, provided the caregivers are able to respond appropriately. If it is attention he need, the child's behavior will be attention-seeking. If they need approval, the behavior will be approval-seeking. And if the child needs discipline his behavior will likely be discipline-seeking. It is as if the child is an actor in a play, hence the term "acting-out." There are some clearly defined patterns of acting-out that not only help children find expressions for their pain but also actually help them to survive. We will discuss these patterns of behavior, better known as survival roles, in greater detail in the next chapter.

As already mentioned, young children do not possess the necessary skills to cope with emotional pain on their own. As with everything else they are dependent on their caretakers for help in grieving. The best children can do is to act-out their pain and hope their parents and other caretakers in their lives are healthy enough to notice the behavior, accurately assess the need, and respond accordingly. When parents possess the skills to respond consistently to their children's needs for time, attention, affection, and direction, they are helping their children resolve the current episode of grief to some extent, as well as to build the internal structures necessary to cope effectively with grief and loss on their own later in life. When parents are not able to respond appropriately to the child's need for help, loss-related wounds tend to accumulate right along with the wounds of abandonment, further complicating the child's pain.

Severe cases of emotional wounding, also known as trauma, results in situations where children have experienced overt abuse or other major losses coupled with inadequate support to aid in their grief. The emotional trauma that comes from abuse violates not only the child's emotional dependency needs but also his most basic needs, the survival dependency needs. This is especially true for their need to feel safe and protected. Imagine a child's dilemma when he needs protection from the very people who are supposed to provide it. The following are some forms of abuse and/or major losses that produce moderate to severe emotional trauma in children:

Sexual and Physical Abuse
Emotional abuse or neglect: Emotionally unavailable parent(s) or parents who give their child the opposite of what they need such as name-calling, belittling, threats of abandonment, shaming, etc.

Psychological abuse: Ignoring the child as if she does not exist or denial of a child's reality such as telling her they didn't see what she saw (e.g., "Daddy wasn't drunk, don't you ever say that again!")

- Frequent Moves
- Adoption Issues
- Prolonged separation from a parent
- Reversal of parent/child roles
- Rigid family rules
- Divorce
- Death of a parent or other family member
- Mentally Ill parent or family member
- Cruel and Unusual punishment: such as locking a child in the closet.

Shame
As discussed in Chapter 1, it is imperative that children feel safe and protected as part of getting their survival needs met. In order to feel safe, even in an unsafe environment, children idealize their caretakers. In other words, little kids put their parents up on a pedestal and see them as perfect, all-knowing

and all-powerful god-like creatures. Idealization is a defense mechanism that helps children feel safe because they get the feeling that nothing can get to them, since they are protected by a god.

Since god-like creatures are perfect, they are beyond reproach in the innocent mind of a child. Children cannot say to themselves, *"Well, Dad has a drinking problem. That's about him not me; I don't have to take it personally when he breaks his promises and yells at me all the time."* No, in the mind of a child it goes more like this... *"If I were a better kid Daddy wouldn't drink."* or *"If I was a better kid Mommy wouldn't yell at me so much."* or the classic, *"Daddy, please don't leave, I'll be good!"*

Because of idealization, young children can make sense of it no other way; it has to be about them. Parents have all the power, and the child has none. They are totally submitted and committed to the parent. Thus, they develop a sense of defectiveness, and it begins to grow along with the wounds. So, if abandonment is an emotional wound, then *shame is an emotional infection* that sets in as the wound goes unattended [see Fig. 3]. This infection has a voice, and it grows stronger as the wounds accumulate. The child's self-talk begins to sound like this, *"No one could ever love me."* *"I don't count."* *"What's wrong with me?"* *"I'm stupid, lazy, unworthy of anyone's attention."*

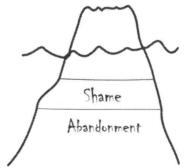

Figure 3: The infection of shame

In a shame-based family system, these internal messages of shame are actually confirmed by the parents. Sometimes the confirmations are more subtle and come in veiled threats of abandonment, double-bind messages, gestures that convey contempt for the child and other nonverbal expressions of disdain. Other times the confirmations are directly stated through name-calling, belittling, and emotional battering such as *"You're stupid, ugly, lazy, fat,"* etc. *"No one could love you." "You can't do anything right."* These messages result in what John Bradshaw (2005) has termed "toxic shame" in his book *Healing the Shame that Binds You.* Of course, these messages frequently come with a misguided positive intention to motivate the child.

The infection of shame exacerbates the wounds of abandonment, and the pain grows. In the worst-case scenarios, such as sexual abuse or incest, toxic shame is a byproduct regardless of the messages a child received before the abuse occurred, or after it ended.

Contempt

In keeping with the analogy of a wound, *contempt is the scab* that forms over the infection of shame and the wound of abandonment [see Fig. 4]. The scab of contempt consists of all the "crusty" feelings of anger, resentment, and bitterness. It is what the child is most aware of, and it skews his whole experience of life as well as his role in it. Some call it the "life sucks" syndrome. The negative energy from the contempt must be directed somewhere. There are two possible choices, and the choice is made at an unconscious level. The energy can be directed inward in the form of self-contempt; or outward as contempt for people, society, authority figures, the opposite sex, or whoever is available, including God.

If we have a tendency to point the contempt inward at self, we are *internalizing* it. If we are more likely to turn it outward toward others, we are *externalizing* the contempt. The self-talk of an Internalizer is all about the defectiveness of self and his or her unworthiness to exist, leading to inappropriate guilt, and more shame, making the emotional infection worse. The self-talk of the Externalizer is all about the defectiveness of others and the unfairness of it all, leading to inappropriate anger.

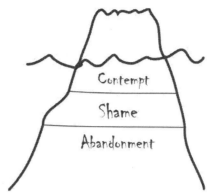

Figure 4: The scab of contempt

Many of us will internalize the contempt until we can't take it anymore and then blow up, directing it outward in an attempt to ventilate. When we externalize or "dump" our contempt it lands on whoever is nearby, usually those who are closest to us. Then, because we have hurt someone we love, we turn the contempt back on ourselves through more shame-based messages such as, *"See there. I've done it again ... I've hurt someone I care about! I've proven it this time ... I really am a loser!"* Internalizing the contempt feeds the infection of shame, speeding up its progression and the power it has over us.

Some people tend to internalize their contempt while others tend to externalize it. People who are primarily Internalizers have problems with depression, caretaking, approval-seeking, lack of adequate boundaries, and lack of a sense of personal power. They have difficulty saying, "no" because that may bring disapproval, which is extremely anxiety-provoking since it is the opposite of what they seek. Persons that are predominantly Externalizers are less likely to be aware of their behavior and the effect it has on others. They believe other people should do things their way, tend to be self-centered, intrusive, have rigid boundaries, may have an excessive need to be right, and proclaim that they don't need anyone.

Externalizers have a tendency to demonstrate what Bradshaw calls *"shameless behavior."* Shameless behavior is seen in situations of abuse where the abuser is exercising god-like control over the victim. Examples of shameless behavior include sexual, physical, and emotional abuse. Shameless Externalizers develop a very thick scab. In the extreme cases, the person involved in shameless behavior is unaware on a conscious level that his behavior is wrong or sometimes even that it is hurtful to the victim. On an unconscious level, Externalizers cannot escape the reality of their behavior or its impact on the victim. The unconscious mind knows all; the shame, guilt, and remorse continue to accumulate for Externalizers, even though they are largely unaware of it. As their infection of shame grows, so does their contempt along with the need to externalize it. This build-up of contempt may eventually lead the Externalizer to episodes of the violent and/or dangerous behavior described earlier in this chapter.

The False Self

The wound of abandonment, the infection of shame, and the scab of contempt forms a free-floating mass of pain just beneath the surface of our awareness which creates in a child a false sense of identity – A False Self [see Fig. 5].

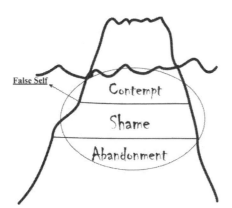

Figure 5: The False Self

The term "False Self" is used because it is just that–false, not true; a counterfeit self. It really feels like who we are, whether we were the child back there-and-then or the adult reading this book here-and-now. But this is not who we really are, and I hope to prove that in a moment. It *feels that way* because the wound is *emotional in nature*. Despite our best efforts, we cannot simply transfer the intellectual reality of this truth to our emotional reality. It is not until significant healing of the emotional wounds takes place that we are able to *feel* differently about ourselves.

Many times we have heard the saying, "kids are resilient." This is likely an effort to minimize our own guilt about not having been able to protect and/or nurture them the way they needed. While it is true that kids are resilient, the implication that they are now fine and have bounced back is not accurate. Emotional wounds do not go away. They must be tended to just like any other wound or the infection grows, and it gets worse. "Kids are survivors" is a more accurate statement. In the next chapter, we begin to explore how a child learns to survive and even get some of her needs met despite difficult circumstances. The skills they learn help them to survive, but they don't go very far in helping them effectively cope with adult life or have an intimate relationship.

Again, if you are a parent, please stay with your feelings about your own childhood experiences as much as possible as you read. Try to avoid getting lost in worry or guilt over your children. There is good news to come. For now, keep in mind that the best way to help them is to help *you* first. They learn by watching what you do, so demonstrate for them how to heal. Yes, get them into counseling if they need it and pay attention to their behavior if they are acting out. However, take care of yourself in the process too.

Chapter 3

The Art of Survival

In order for children to survive the pain of their wounds they must learn to live outside themselves; i.e., they must develop an *external focus* [see Fig. 6]. In other words, the child must find distractions in their outer world to avoid the pain of their inner world. Everything outside of our own skin is our outer world, while our thoughts and feelings exist only in our inner world. We experience our feelings in our body while our thoughts are located in our mind.

External Focus

Children develop this external focus through a number of distractions such as imaginary friends, relationships with pets or stuffed animals, watching cartoons, and staying busy with play. Later the distraction may be video games, skateboarding, or sports. Kids who have a lot of pain have difficulty with inactivity and quite time. One will often hear them proclaim, *"I'm bored! I can't stand boredom!"*

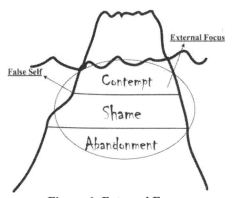

Figure 6: External Focus

In my work with teenagers, I encountered the "I can't stand boredom" syndrome many times before I learned that it really is true for some. Many kids have trouble tolerating boredom not because of boredom itself, but because of what boredom represents to them. Boredom to these wounded kids is a red flag. It's a signal that they are losing their external focus. As their attention begins to drift inward, anxiety starts to build because the next thing to come into their awareness would be their emotional pain. It rarely gets that far because the children or teenagers are compelled to take action to help them regain their external focus. A common scenario follows:

> Billy, a teenager, is referred to counseling for habitually skipping school. Through the counseling process, it is discovered that this child's father is alcoholic and that things at home are fairly chaotic most of the time. In order to keep an external focus and avoid his emotional pain, Billy has to remain actively involved and interested in class. However, every day, right after lunch Billy has a math class. He is not interested in math at all because he is not very good at it (competence issue) so it is only a short time before "boredom" sets in.
>
> Billy tries to regain his external focus by staring out the window in a daydream. That works for about three minutes. Soon, he finds himself passing notes, shooting spitballs, or talking to his neighbor. Before long, the teacher is involved in disciplining Billy, again, for disrupting the classroom. Billy then gets into an argument with his teacher, who is "always picking on me" (externalization of contempt). The teacher takes him out into the hall where the next external focus, the principal, is approaching.
>
> Billy has the option of going through this routine or avoiding it altogether by skipping the class. The easiest option is to skip class and find some way to regain his external focus. Sometimes he would get a friend to sneak off with him to go to hangout downtown, or he would sneak off onto the parking lot to drink or do drugs, or simply go home to watch videos, play on the Internet, or engage in some other distraction.

Acting-out is only one method that helps children distract from their emotional pain. Again, other methods include creating imaginary friends, having relationships with stuffed animals or pets, video games, comic books, cartoons, hyperactivity, and various other ways to stay outside of themselves.

Invented Self

Another thing a child must do in order to avoid her inner world and stay in her outer world is to unconsciously build a wall between her awareness and her unawareness. These "walls" are constructed automatically of psychological defense mechanisms and have been collectively referred to as *"survival roles"* because their function is to help children survive in the face of unmet dependency needs. Children learn to "cover up" their false self by projecting an image other people might find acceptable. This is often referred to as "wearing a mask." I think of it as inventing a self [see Fig. 7] to cover up the false self because, "If people really knew me they would not like me (shame), and they would reject me (fear of more abandonment)."

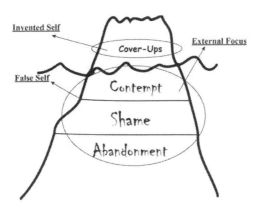

Figure 7: Invented Self

Children unwittingly invent and project these images, or survival roles, through the use of unconscious defense mechanisms in order to avoid the intolerable reality of their unmet needs. The pain is still there, but it is not as "in their face" as it would be due to one defense known as repression.

Repression automatically pushes the pain deep into their subconscious until the child matures, and heals, enough to develop the psychological equipment to cope with it.

Survival roles also serve to help the child find ways to get her needs for time, attention, affection, and direction met. For example, in a dysfunctional family one parent gets caught up in some form of problematic behavior while the other gets caught up with trying to control or "fix" the problem parent. They get enmeshed with each other and the problem behavior while leaving less and less time to attend to anything else, including the children.

Family Hero:

When the first child comes along, he or she finds out fairly quickly that in order to get any time, attention, affection, and direction in this family he or she has to do something outstanding to get noticed. So this child usually becomes the *Hero*. There are two kinds of family heroes. The first is the flashy hero who gets all A's, is captain of the football team, valedictorian, class president, head cheerleader or a combination of the above. The second type is the behind-the-scenes hero; aka the *Responsible One* or the *Parentified Child*. This is the child who comes home from school early every day, does the laundry, gets the mail, prepares dinner, does the dishes, takes care of the younger kids and, in essence, becomes a parent at ten years old.

Rebel/Scapegoat:

The second child usually becomes the *Rebel* or *Scapegoat*. They can rarely compete with the first child for the positive attention because the Hero has a head start. So the Rebel must settle for the next-best thing, i.e., negative attention. The Rebel gets time, attention, affection, and direction from teachers, principals, juvenile officers, counselors and anyone else who would try to help them. While they may not get the positive attention, they do end up getting the most attention. The parents must stop what they are doing to deal with this kid's misbehavior because the school or juvenile office keeps calling.

Lost Child:

The third child cannot compete for the positive attention or the negative attention, so they don't get any attention and become the *Lost Child*. In order to survive, this child relies on fantasy to get her needs partially met. An example of a Lost Child is the seven-year-old girl who is always somewhere in the background playing with a doll that she has had forever. One hardly ever notices that she is even there. She says nice things to the doll, combs its hair, tucks her in every night, rocks her to sleep and, in essence, creates a family of her own, vicariously getting her needs met by becoming a nurturing parent to the doll. The Lost Child may also have anywhere from eight to twelve stuffed animals on her bed at one time and knows each of them intimately. This child spends so much time in her fantasy world that she loses out on opportunities to make friends in the real world.

Family Mascot:

The fourth child, usually the *Mascot*, is the baby of the family. This child gets his needs met through being on stage. He or she is the class clown or the beauty queen. This child's job is to bring entertainment to the family, usually in the form of humor.

The roles described above are the classic survival roles described by Sharon Wegscheider-Cruse (1991) in her book *The Family Trap*. These roles do not always follow the pattern described above, but considerably more often than not, they do. The firstborn is usually the Hero because it is the preferred role, and the child has the first crack at it. All kids want the positive attention and honor assigned to the Hero. However, if that mask is taken, then the next children have to settle for the next-best thing. The Rebel is the second most effective role. Even though the attention is negative, they get lots more of it because the parents have to deal with this child's misbehavior, so the Rebel becomes the priority. Middle children are more like to get lost in the crowd, so they must sharpen their skills with fantasy in order to survive. These children also tend to be chameleons, switching from one survival role to another whenever the opportunity presents itself. Many times they experience all the roles in their life at one time or another. The baby of the family is almost always the center of attention so it is not surprising that these children make the most of that and become the Mascot.

So, it is *birth order, not personality, not willfulness, and not inherently bad character* that reinforces or "shapes" the original masks we learn to wear. Children do not decide to behave this way, they instinctively act-out these roles until they find the one that works the best in getting them the time, attention, affection and direction they need. Heroes get it from teachers, coaches, newspaper reporters, and others who are amazed by their outstanding abilities. Rebels gets it from teachers, principals, juvenile officers, counselors, and anyone else who wants to help them get back on track. The Lost Child gets it through fantasy, and the Mascot gets it through being on stage.

These roles are also reinforced at home because they all bring something to the family, helping the system to survive as well. The Hero brings honor to the family. The Rebel brings distraction, which takes the focus off the primary dysfunction in the marital pair. This is why another term used for the Rebel is "Scapegoat." They act as a lightning rod help to keep the family intact because, if the parents have too much time to face what is going on between them, they might get a divorce, and the family then disintegrates. The Lost Child brings relief because you never have to worry about this child and hardly notice he is there. The Mascot brings entertainment and humor, diffusing the seriousness of the family dysfunction. All of these roles look different on the outside, but they are all alike on the inside.

Impression Management

Another function of the Invented Self is to manage the impressions of others that are important to us. Impression Management is driven by the "what-would-other-people-think" syndrome. It goes something like this: If I have ten people in my life who are important to me, and one of them is not happy with me while the other nine think I am the greatest thing in the world, I would focus much of my energy thinking about how I could get that one back in line with the others. If two or three get upset with me, I get anxious. If four or five of them don't think much of me, I get disparate or panicky because it almost feels like I am dying.

It feels like I am dying because, in a way, I am. I draw my identity, my sense of self, from those ten people. Hence, I must be vigilant in managing the impressions of those around me. If they accept me and think I am okay then I must be … right? Not necessarily—even if they accept me—I cannot truly accept their acceptance because, at another level, I feel like a phony. An example of this is when we have difficulty accepting compliments from others. Somewhere inside the voice of shame is telling us *"They wouldn't say that if they really knew you!"* The voice may even be inaudible, but we feel like a phony anyway. This accounts for the paradox of why we tend to discount or minimize anything positive coming from those we try to please.

The survival roles described above are examples of the masks we learn to wear in childhood. As we grow and the pain continues to accumulate, we get more and more sophisticated in the masks we wear. For a fairly complete catalog of masks read John Powell's book (1995) *Why I am afraid to tell you who I am.*

Chapter 4

Who Am I Really?

As we have seen, the *False Self* is just that–false. It is an emotional wound and, like any other wound, it has gotten infected due to lack of attention. The severity of the wound of abandonment and the infection of shame are hard to see because they are covered by the scab of contempt, and for the most part, it is out of our awareness. We have also seen that our *Invented Self* is not who we are either. The False Self poses as our private self and the Invented Self as our public self, but both are imposters or counterfeits–so who are we really? For anyone who has ever struggled with addiction, codependency, and/or dysfunctional relationships, that is the million-dollar question.

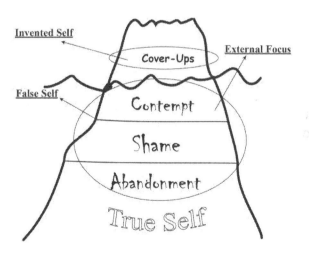

Figure 8: True Self

I mentioned in Chapter 2 that I think I can prove to the reader that the False Self is not who we really are. I know I can prove it to some, and I think I can prove it to others, but I am not sure I can prove it to all. Here goes: If you believe there is a Divine Creator, do you think He would want a small child to feel defective at her very core? Would a loving God want children to go through their entire childhood feeling rotten through and through? That everything bad that happens is their fault? Of course not!

This is proof *for believers* that the False Self is *not* what God created. No, these emotional wounds *are what life created*. The *True Self* is what God created, and it has been with us in our inner world since before we were born. Then life happened. The wounds grew and covered up the True Self, pushing it far beneath the surface of our awareness before we even had a chance to get to know ourselves. It was replaced with an imposter; as a child we bought it and learned to live outside ourselves, abandoning our inner world. Then we poured a slab of concrete over it (Invented Self), locking it all in place and effectively alienating ourselves from who we were created to be [Fig. 8].

It is my belief that the True Self is who God created and that this is where our spirit resides. I also believe this is why God feels especially far away to some. Our spirit is what connects with his Spirit. To the extent that we don't have access to our spirit, we feel cut-off from God. Our True Self is also where our purpose resides. In Rick Warren's book, *A Purpose-Driven Life* (2002, 2007), the author points out that our purpose is not really *our* purpose at all … it is *His* purpose for us. We were created with a special set of talents and abilities in order to perform His purpose for us.

In the Bible, it says that *"He who overcomes himself is greater than he who overcomes a city."* Do you wonder which "self" we are to overcome? In another place, the Bible says, *"Blessed are those who mourn: for they shall be comforted."* Is *refusing to mourn* not what we do when we wear a mask, ignore our inner world, and pretend that everything is fine? When God feels far away, could it be because our True Self, the part of us that connects with him, is buried so deep under the wounds of the False Self that we cannot feel his presence? If the answers to these questions are "yes," then turning our focus inward to surface and grieve our pain is the royal road to *true comfort and relief*. As we shall see in the next chapter, seeking comfort and relief in all the wrong places inevitably leads to more pain.

Even if you are agnostic, or atheist, for that matter, I think most can believe in the innocence of a child. We all come into this world innocent and pure. That innocent, pure True Self gets wounded and covered up by this world regardless of your religious or spiritual beliefs. For those of you who believe neither in God, nor in the inherent goodness of man, I may not have been able to provide sufficient proof of the True Self. If not, I challenge you to look within and see if it might be contempt and emotional wounds that are getting in your way. I believe in you and wish you all the wonderful things that life has to offer.

The next logical questions are, *"How do we deal with this? How do we uncover our True Self?"* The good news is that there are answers to these questions. The bad news is that we first have more pain and consequences of emotional trauma to explore before we can answer them.

Chapter 5

Illusions of Comfort and Relief
Pain as a Motivator

As already pointed out, the role of pain in our life is to motivate us to do something different. Pain lets us know that what we are doing is not working by signaling that we are moving further away from happiness. It is a warning system that tells us when something is wrong or when something needs attention. Remember the formula from Chapter 1, A → B? This formula is not rocket science so why do we keep doing the same things over and over expecting a different outcome each time? The easiest answer to that question is *because we don't know what else to do*. We are all doing our best to achieve that one ultimate goal in life, to be happy. Perhaps happiness eludes us due to the progressively dysfunctional methods we unwittingly rely upon to feel better. Soon the best we can hope for is comfort and relief.

We don't like pain and when we encounter it, we are compelled to seek comfort and relief. Growing up with all of this woundedness is painful. So where do we find comfort and relief? We cannot generate any good feelings on the inside because we can't even go there, it is too painful. So, we must look to things outside of us for comfort and relief. Since we are all genetically and psychologically "wired" a little differently, we will find one or two things that "really does it" for us. Some of us are wired for alcohol or other drugs, others for excessive working, spending, drama, risk-taking, sexing, gambling, eating, and others for addictive relationships. These are only a few of the distractions available to us in this candy store we call America [Fig. 9]

Emotional Attachments

When we find the object or event that "really does it for us" then we attach to it on an emotional level because *we love what it does for us*. It provides us with a very powerful, instantaneous, although short-lived feeling. Soon *we begin to trust the object or event* because it does what it is supposed to do (make us feel better) very quickly, very powerfully; in a way no one and nothing else can – every single time we ask it to. So, we attach to the object or event on an emotional level.

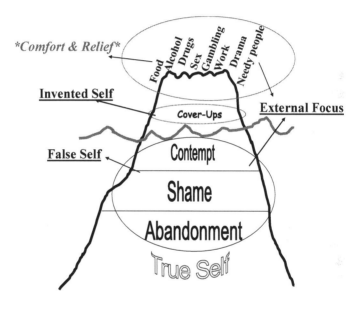

Figure 9: Comfort and Relief

Love and trust are the main ingredients for a primary relationship. This emotional attachment signals the beginning of a serious problem because we are not supposed to have primary relationships with objects and events. Our primary relationships are supposed to be with people who are important to us. Craig Nakken defines addiction in his book, *The Addictive Personality*. According to Nakken, addiction is, "a pathological relationship with an object or event that produces a desired mood swing." This is, in my opinion, the best definition of addiction I have heard. I do, however, take the liberty of making one minor distinction for the benefit of my clients. I define addiction as *"an unhealthy primary relationship with an object or event that produces a desired mood swing."* I make this distinction for a couple of reasons. First of all, "pathological" seems to produce more stigma than "unhealthy" even though they mean the same thing. Secondly, "primary" highlights why the relationship is unhealthy.

Most people don't realize and will, in fact, initially deny that they have such a strong emotional attachment to their addiction of choice. In both treatment groups and individual sessions, I have asked my addicted clients the following question for the past several years, always with the same results: *"What is the most important relationship in your life?"* They will respond with *"My wife, my kids, my mom, my boyfriend or girlfriend."* I always just shake my head and say *"Wrong answer."* They initially get a little indignant that I would be so presumptuous to assume I know what is more important to them than they do themselves. Then all I have to say is *"When was the last time you lied to your mom about ..., broke a promise to your kids about ..., broke up with a girlfriend over... etc."* There is rarely an argument. I close this discussion with *"Maybe in your heart, they are most important to you, but in your life the reality is that the addiction trumps everything else."*

Let's look for a moment at the implications of this emotional attachment to an object or event. First of all, the question of "choice" frequently comes up. For example, "He chose to start; he can choose to stop!" This attachment is a love and trust relationship just like any other love and trust relationship. When was the last time you "chose" to fall in love with someone? How easy is it to end a relationship with someone you love, even when you know it is for the best? When you do end such a relationship you can expect to grieve. Since this is one of the most important relationships in your life the grief process kicks in full-steam when one decides to get help and give up their addiction. This is manageable if we have the internal coping skills and external support network to manage the pain of this "letting-go" process. However, if we have this unhealthy primary relationship in the first place that implies that we have neither the skills nor the support necessary to manage the pain associated with this loss. So we fall back on the object or activity that we trust the most. This is precisely why people relapse into their addiction and precisely how they eventually lose their "choice" to "just quit." To make matters worse, in some cases, there is the physical pain of withdrawal to contend with as well.

The comfort we achieve through this relationship with an object or event is an illusion. Remember, the wounds we must relieve in order to be happy is *emotional in nature*. Therefore, we need emotional comfort and relief, such as the kind we get when our basic needs are met, in order to heal and be healthy. The "comfort and relief" we achieve through the use of our object or event of choice is not emotional but physiological or *physical in nature*. In other words, we learn to mask our emotional pain with "medicine." That means any time we have a feeling we don't like, we medicate it rather than listen to it, understand it, and respond to it. This just pushes the feeling back down inside to accumulate with the pain that is already there. Using a chemical to medicate our emotional pain is tantamount to masking a serious back injury with painkillers while we go on working. We keep doing more and more damage without realizing it because our "warning system" (pain) was taken out of the way. Thus we continue to do things to increase our shame, guilt, contempt, and remorse. We prove it over and over again, that "we can't do anything right." We eventually abandon our money, our families, our cars, our pride, our careers, our dreams, our goals, ourselves, etc. As our pain increases, so does our need for "comfort and relief" [Fig. 10].

Sooner or later we will crash and "hit bottom" [Fig. 11]. This happens when we have accumulated so much pain that there is not enough "comfort and relief" to offset it anymore. The "coping skill" that used to work instantly now only barely works. This is when we are using just to feel normal. Some addictions get us there faster than others. Some addictions are too easy to hide. For instance, if we are addicted to alcohol, we can get a DWI or DUI, but if we have an addiction to work, we get a bonus.

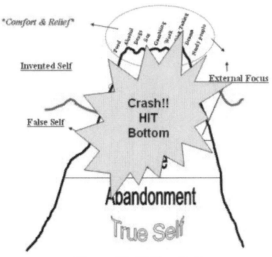

Figure 10: Hitting Bottom

Hitting Bottom

A major obstacle to hitting bottom are the well-intentioned others who enable us by interfering with the A → B formula mentioned earlier. People who love and care about us want to help when we are in trouble. For example, when we do "A" (spend our rent money on alcohol) we should receive "B" (have to deal with it ourselves–i.e., take on extra work to pay the rent or be evicted). However, when someone steps in and gives us "C" (pays our rent for us "this time") instead of letting us experience "B" they have become our enabler. "Enablers" helps maintain our addiction a little longer by reducing or eliminating our pain. Remember, pain is a motivator and teacher. "Tough Love" means stepping out of the way and letting us experience "B." Often times our chief enabler is just as wounded as we are, so we have become his external focus. Think about it, what better way to distract from our own problems than to find a "problem person" to focus on. We tend to choose people on an unconscious as well as a conscious level. This explains how many people end up getting out of one bad relationship only to find that they are right back in another. Such people have an excessive need to be needed. They are Internalizers who find comfort and relief from becoming important to others. You will often hear other people say about them, *"What a saint of a woman! Look at all she goes through, and still she sticks with him!"* The masks they wear include the Martyr, The Rescuer, and the Victim.

Until we do get our wake-up call, unconscious psychological defenses block acceptance of the reality and extent of our addiction. Examples are: *Rationalization* (Excuse making, justifying); *Projection* (Blaming anything and anyone except the real problem); *Minimizing* (It's not that bad, I can quit anytime I want); *Diversion Tactics* (debating, arguing, withdrawing, and changing the subject); *Disarming* (That's just the way I am), *Hostility* (Intimidating others who try to talk about it); etc.

When the "call" does come, we are likely to reach out for help. The irony of this is that many people who reach out for help with their pain don't really want to know what's bothering them because their denial is still intact. They just know they want comfort and relief. For those readers who need help, I hope that this book will raise your bottom to the point you get it sooner than later. Unfortunately, some have a very high tolerance for pain, and they wait too long and some tragedy strikes. You don't have to wait until that happens. It is not easy, but with honesty, open-mindedness, and willingness you can recover!

Chapter 6

The Twilight Zone

Recovery from addiction is easy–*all you have to do is change your whole life*.

The transition from the old life to the new is a period of limbo where the past is too painful to return to and the future is too uncertain to feel comfortable about. There is much to be done, and it cannot be done all at once. If people plunge headlong into their emotional pain, they will be compelled to seek comfort and relief in the only way they know how which results in a relapse into their addiction of choice. The first thing one must do is give up his comfort and relief [Fig. 12], accept that he cannot recover alone, and reach out to others for help. For these reasons, the *pain of not reaching out* for help must outweigh the *pain of continuing to engage* in the addiction.

Figure 12: Giving Up Comfort

Reaching Out

Reaching out to others is an interpersonal skill that we are not born with. *Acting out* is the instinct children are born with in order to express their needs. If we grew up with a significant amount of emotional pain then we are not likely to be very good at reaching out because it was either not taught or not allowed. Furthermore, the infection of shame makes it very difficult to ask for help. Often, it is only when the pain grows to an unbearable proportion that we begin to consider reaching out. Adding the accumulated shame of our entire life with having to admit a problem with alcohol, drugs, sex, food, or gambling, to name a few, gives us an idea of the magnitude of the problem one can have with asking for help. Can you hear the voice of shame? *"See, now you are really proving what a loser you are!"*

Reaching out requires a certain amount of self-disclosure, i.e. taking off the mask of the Invented-Self. The need to manage the impressions of others cries out to keep quiet and find some other way to work this out. This is the primary reason that such value is placed upon the anonymity of members of 12-Step groups. They realize the importance of safety to those newcomers who may be considering reaching out by attending a meeting for the first time. Even when the pain is great enough to bring someone in for counseling, they are compelled to manage the impression of the counselor to the extent that it can actually sabotage the assessment process. Here people who have "reached out" by making the counseling appointment will answer many of the questions in a way that suggests they are fine and there really is no problem. Sometimes it takes a few sessions before they begin to feel safe enough with the helper, the environment, and the confidentiality to open up.

Internalizers are a little more likely to reach out early than Externalizers because the latter have an excessive need to be right. Externalizers are "shameless" because their defenses are geared toward making everyone else responsible for their problems. To admit a problem of any kind requires taking an inward look. This is highly irregular for an Externalizer because her shamelessness is in proportion to the actual shame and pain she would feel if she could see the truth. So, again, the pain of hitting bottom must outweigh the pain of facing her inner world before she is motivated to reach out.

On the other hand, the defenses of Internalizers are geared toward self-contempt. They are "not important, never right about anything, total failures, and unworthy of happiness." These are the very depressing thoughts of an Internalizer which make him already depressed even before the wake-up call comes. Again, most people are rarely at one end of the contempt continuum or the other, although there are some cases in which this is true. More often, we have a tendency to slide up and down on that line internalizing for as long as we can stand it then blowing up occasionally to externalize, or dump, some of that contempt.

When people do feel enough pain to come in for help many times their denial is still largely intact. They may say, "I am here to get help with my depression." The therapist might ask, "Why are you depressed?" Client: "I don't know." Therapist: "Well, do you drink?" Client: "Yes, but that's not my concern right now." Therapist: "How much and how often do you drink?" Client, "Probably too much, I have had three DUIs, but that's not why I am here. I came because I am depressed." Therapist: "If that is not the problem then do you have any theories about what is?" Client, "You're the therapist, you tell me!"

This person is still looking for ways to avoid giving up his unhealthy primary relationship with alcohol. He wants help to find comfort and relief but is still fighting that painful inward look. He is already in pain and to let go of his denial too soon might be overwhelming. Care must be taken to go forward at an acceptable pace building coping skills and supports first. If one is to give up their primary coping skill, they must have something to replace it with prior to doing to work ahead. Even then, it gets worse before it gets better.

People who reach out later than sooner are usually so full of shame that when they do take that initial inward look, they say things like, *"Man, I don't even have any values anymore!"* I had one person tell me they felt that they had actually become evil. In addition to the toxic shame, what they have become emotionally infected with is the normal guilt and remorse they feel for the bad things they have done during their addiction.

The food addict is full of shame over repeated failures to control eating. The sex addict is full of shame over the inability to honor the marriage by staying faithful. The gambling addict is full of shame over the inability to take care of his family due to overwhelming debt. The work-a-holic is full of shame over hundreds of broken promises to spend time with his wife and kids.

Recovery – A Hard Sell

Imagine you are reaching out for help because you are in the most emotional pain you have ever felt. Now imagine hearing the helper say that you need to give up the only comfort and relief you've ever known and face this pain [Fig. 12]. That's what it is like for someone who finds himself at the bottom. It is a very hard sell even when the person knows you are right. Along with reaching out, abstinence is another of the first things we need to accomplish if we are going to heal.

At this point, some simple definitions are in order. *Abstinence* means not engaging in *any* unhealthy relationships with objects or events to produce a desired mood swing. Many times people give up their addiction of choice only to begin relying on another unhealthy relationship to medicate their pain. Alcoholics may switch to marijuana; sex addicts may switch to gambling, gambling addicts to drinking, compulsive spenders to food, etc. This is called *substitution* because we are simply substituting *one unhealthy relationship for another*. It's like a rebound relationship; how long are we likely to stay with our second choice when we know our first choice is waiting in the wings? This is a strategy many people employ even before they get to the point of needing to reach out. It doesn't work because it only addresses the need for comfort and relief. The rest of The Iceberg remains intact. Sooner or later the emotional pain flares up again and the substitute just doesn't get it. *Cross-addiction* is what happens when the substitute *does do just as much* for us as the unhealthy relationship of choice. But now we have two addictions to overcome because the new one almost always leads back to the old one.

Abstinence is a required task in order for recovery to take place. How does one abstain from food addictions, sex addiction, work addictions, and spending addictions? Abstinence in these cases means using the objects and events only in the healthy ways for which they are intended. This means we eat for the right reasons, we have sex for the right reasons with the right person, we balance work with the other areas of our lives, and we spend for the right reasons. We avoid self-medicating while improving emotional coping skills, building a support network, learning how to communicate, and healing the internal wounds.

Prescription for Recovery

Recovery means abstaining and liking it better than engaging in unhealthy relationships with objects or events. The only way we are going to like abstinence better than engaging in our addictions is when we find comfort from the internal healing that begins to take place. This healing can only occur through the development of healthy recovery-oriented behaviors and activities.

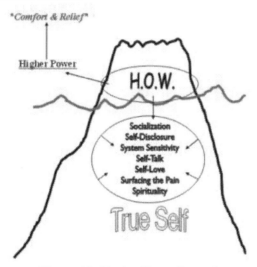

Figure 13: Turing Focus Inward

In the 12-Step groups, suggested recovery activities are:
- Go to Recovery Meetings
- Get a Sponsor
- Pray and Meditate
- Read Recovery Literature
- Practice the 12 Steps of Recovery

In his Video *Shame and Addiction* John Bradshaw suggests:

Socialization – Attend non-shaming recovery or church groups
- Self-Disclosure – Come out of hiding, break the no-talk rule
- System Sensitivity – Understand the family system you came from
- Self-Talk – Positive affirmations
- Self-Love – Take care of yourself
- Surfacing the Pain – Talk about it, understand it, get it out
- Spirituality – Prayer and Meditation

Relapse means undoing recovery enough to be able to return to an unhealthy relationship. Relapse is a process that ends when we re-engage our addictive relationship of choice. One cannot relapse without a period of recovery. A period of abstinence with no recovery activities is called stopping. "Stopping" is easy; staying stopped is the hard part. Stopping is always followed by starting again. This is why a good friend of mine in recovery likes to say, *"I can't stop drinking because if I stop, I know I will start again."* He reminds himself and others, "I can abstain one day at a time by the grace of a power greater than myself."

What Next?
As mentioned throughout this book, arresting addictions, codependency, chronic depression, and other long-term life

problems is a critical piece, but it is only the *"tip of the Iceberg."* Stabilizing these conditions through the development of healthy coping skills and a good support network is the foundation for the work that lies ahead. Many people recover through the use of the 12-Step programs and other community support programs alone. Some people speed the healing process up with the inclusion of therapy as part of their recovery program.

However, what about that one ultimate goal that we all have in common—that state of being that we all pursue so vigorously? I have found that happiness–i.e., *contentment, fulfillment, satisfaction, wholeness and completeness*, is not something we can seek and find. It is a byproduct of living the way we were intended to live—as our True Self [Fig. 14]. Codependency, chronic depression, Adult/Child Syndrome, and the many other long-term consequences of abandonment, shame and contempt are OPTIONAL. You don't have to live that way anymore. If you feel ready now, begin working on Part I of the *Thawing the Iceberg* recovery program in the following pages.

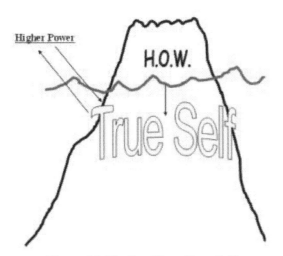

Figure 14: Finding Your True Self

Thawing
Childhood Abandonment Issues

The Workbook

Important Recommendations:

The program contained in the following pages contains **"Audio Alerts."** These are sections that alert the reader/listener to stop reading and use one of a series of audio exercises designed to assist in connecting with the issues of each stage of child development. The audios contain exercises that will help to initiate a healing process for each stage. While not required, these audios provide the "experiential" component of the **Thawing Childhood Abandonment Issues Program**.

For maximum benefit, it is highly recommended that the reader acquire the audios and use them. They can be purchased at **www.Internet-of-the-Mind.com** or by email: **dcarter73@msn.com** (See Appendix A for more details). It is also recommended that a separate journal or diary be used to do the written work. A sketchpad for the drawing exercises is also recommended but not required.

Introduction:

Figure 15: "Contempt Continuum"

In *Thawing Childhood Abandonment Issues,* we explore our "inner landscape" in more detail by looking briefly at what the writer believes to be the origins of the *Internalizer* and *Externalizer* of what I refer to in the Iceberg model as a "scab of contempt," referred to elsewhere as Co-dependent and Counter-dependent tendencies. We explore how these roles can be seen developing right alongside of the first six of Erik Erikson's *Eight Stages of Human Development.*

We also look for other symptoms of unmet developmental needs evident in present day situations and relationships. We conclude each section with exercises and activities designed to help heal and release blocked emotions from each stage.

The wounding process occurred during the normal stages of childhood development causing emotional injuries and deficits at each stage. Accordingly, *Thawing Childhood Abandonment Issues* is designed as a ***developmental recovery process*** which treats each stage sequentially, from stage one to six, so that healing can occur in a similar process as the injuries – *developmentally* – healing at one stage will provide the foundation for healing at the next.

Upon completion of the tasks in this book, it is recommended to cycle back through them later on (especially the stages most relevant for the reader) Revisiting them in recursive loops, with a break to integrate new learning, can produce even more healing each time through. This recursive pattern is designed to mimic another developmental process of human growth known as "recycling."

Codependents as "Internalizers":

People who have *disowned or cut themselves off from their Angry/Defiant Child ego-state* tend to get caught up in the **Internalizer** role – such as those who were not allowed to express anger outwardly or perhaps a parent was abusive and a *rage-a-holic* so that it was dangerous to express your anger.

Counter-Dependents as "Externalizers":

Those who have *disowned or cut themselves off from their Vulnerable Child ego-state* tend to gravitate toward the **Externalizer** position – such as those who were not allowed to have their feelings and families where vulnerable feelings were considered "weak."

Healthy, Positive Outcomes:

Those who had a predominantly positive outcome to this and all other stages are able to own and experience both their Angry/Defiant Child and their Vulnerable/Needy Child ego-states *from an integrated position* – i.e., because they have not been emotionally wounded, these two essential elements of self are simultaneously active and working together in harmony.

Before You Begin:

Before you begin, there are several considerations and instructions listed below:

1. First Things First – If you are actively involved in an addictive process this will sabotage your efforts to complete this program. It is essential to meet with an addiction specialist if there is even a hint that you may be using an object (alcohol, drugs, food, etc.) or an activity (sex, gambling, caretaking, etc.) addictively. It is highly recommended that you get an evaluation, follow recommendations, and find a support group of others who are recovering from the same or similar issues. A 12-Step group is proven as the most successful in dealing with addictions.

Once you have achieved Transition and Stabilization and are at least a full year into recovery, you will be ready to begin this program. Beginning this work too soon may trigger strong emotions that could lead to relapse into your addiction. For more information on this issue read the chapter "Distractions and Dependencies" in *THAW – Freedom from Frozen Feelings.*

2. Create a Safe Container – One must create a "safe container" in which to do the necessary "feelings work." This means having a support network of people who know what you are going through such as a therapist, a support group such as Adult Children of Dysfunctional Families or Codependents Anonymous, a sponsor, safe, supportive friends, and/or safe, supportive family members. This work triggers strong emotions which is something most of us have been programmed to avoid. We will need to create safe, supportive relationships so that we can practice emotional health.

It is also necessary to create a safe container at home to do the work – A place where the door can be closed, with a comfortable place to sit, a place to write and a device (with headphones) that plays MP3 files or CDs.

3. Understand and Plan for "Triggers" – A trigger is anything that has been linked or associated with our emotional wounds so that when the trigger is present it activates the abandonment, shame, and contempt which in turn leads to a behavioral reaction. When we get triggered, usually one of two things happen – either we get flooded with strong feelings (emotional flooding), or we go emotionally numb (psychic numbing). In other words we may feel too much or not at all. The numbing is a method the unconscious mind uses to manage the feelings. Flooding occurs when the "walls" holding the feelings back collapse for the moment (repression). Neither of these will cause "the roof to cave in" nor "the world to end," but it may feel like it with flooding. This is why a safe container of safe relationships is essential. Triggers are not to be avoided because "feelings work" is a critical part of healing – it's like emotional surgery, the pain has to come out.

4. Easy Does It, But Do it – Pacing yourself is an important thing to learn as well. If a runner pushes the body too hard, for too long, an injury will eventually occur. We have to "listen to our body" and not push it too hard or we will just be inflicting more abuse on ourselves. Plan for 30 to 45 minutes at a time, four or five days a week if possible. Then try that pace and adjust it according to what you feel is right for you. Or you may want to do an hour and a half on the weekends. Find out what works for you and develop a routine. Yes, it will take some time – maybe even a few months – to complete the work. But rushing through it will do more harm than good.

5. Use a Journal – Invest in a journal, as there are lots of things you will be able to use it for, such as the journaling process in chapter twelve of *THAW – Freedom from Frozen Feelings*. You may also want to record your progress, explore ideas or observations that come up during the work, and write about feelings and experiences that occur along the way.

6. Developmental Recovery Process – This program is designed to be a developmental recovery process to mirror the way the original wounds occurred in the context of childhood developmental stages. In other words, we begin by treating stage one and carry that healing into stage two, then carry the healing from both of those stages into stage three – the healing of one stage sets the foundation for the next in the same way the original wounding process occurred.

7. Audio Alerts – Throughout the program you will find "Audio Alerts." At these times, stop writing and listen to the program indicated in the alert. The audio programs are most effective if listened to at least twice and in some cases three or more times. Recurring loops help one go deeper into the experience which is the goal of using the audios – to "experience" the issues and healing process on a deeper level than can be achieved by reading and writing.

Final Preparations:

a. ***THAW – Freedom from Frozen Feeling-States*** – If you haven't already done so, it is highly useful to read my book *THAW – Freedom from Frozen Feelings* before beginning.

b. ***Thawing Adult/Child Syndrome*** – It is also recommended that your review and complete the *Thawing Adult/Child Syndrome* prior to this work.

c. **[Audio Alert]** Listen to Program *1 Majestic Meadow*

d. **[Audio Alert]** Listen to Program *2 Timeline Discovery* (at least twice)

e. **[Audio Alert]** Listen to Program *3 Ego-States, Sanctuary, & True Self*

f. **Faith & Spirituality** – If you are a person of faith, it is a good time to send out a few prayers asking for guidance and healing with this process.

Stage One - Basic Trust vs. Mistrust
Infancy (0-2 years old)

Infants are totally dependent on their caretakers to meet their needs. Being helpless and unable to communicate needs is the backdrop against which the crisis of infancy is played out. In this child development stage, the only way an infant can express a need is to cry. Initially, they have one type of cry in their repertoire but, though experience, develop different types of cries to signal different needs.

Attentive parents come to recognize these signals quickly. In this way, the signals are established and reinforced – learning is already taking place! It's in how these signals are responded to that the developmental crisis occurs. Parents who notice, evaluate, and respond to the child's needs appropriately and consistently help the child have a positive outcome to this child development stage.

Parents who consistently don't notice the signals, evaluate them incorrectly, or otherwise respond inappropriately, foster a negative outcome for the child. The operative word here is "consistently" – there is plenty of room for mistakes and new, inexperienced parents will make their share of them.

Key Point: Loving and parenting are NOT necessarily the same thing – parenting is a skill. For various reasons, many loving parents do not possess parenting skills adequate to meet the needs of their children… usually because their own parents did not possess adequate parenting skills.

Wounded parents or parents who were not adequately parented themselves will consistently respond with poor parenting skills such as making the same mistakes over and over, miss or simply ignore the signals, or flat out abuse their baby by yelling, shaking, or spanking the infant. Just as infants are not able to ask for what they need, in this stage of development, they are not able to understand direct verbal communication from those who try to meet their needs. Most of what is communicated from a parent to a child comes primarily through three sensory systems – sight, sound, and touch.

Touch is one of the most important sensory channels for babies. The largest sense organ in the body is the skin. Infants experience skin hunger. An incredible amount of data is shared through how the baby is held, stroked, and touched. Positive and negative outcomes for this stage hinge on the type, amount, and frequency of touch. Of course, consistently negative, rigid, infrequent, unloving, fearful, or abusive touch results in negative outcomes in the child development stage of infancy. Alternatively, loving, frequent, soft, nurturing, attentive, and affectionate touch results in positive outcomes.

The "primal gaze" is often observed between mother and infant. This is another incredibly important communication channel from a parent to a child. Does the gaze occur? If so, what messages are being sent to the child? Are the parents' facial expressions loving, adoring, and protective or do they tend to be impatient, harsh, glaring, burdened, etc.?

The qualities of sound are also a major factor – soft, loving, cooing, gentle and confident tones are better for infants than sudden loud noises, yelling, screaming, and harsh tones.

All three of these sensory systems, combined with taste and smell, are active during the most intimate and important connection of all – nursing the infant. There is a little controversy over the issue of bottle feeding vs. breast feeding an infant. However, this issue focuses primarily on physical nourishment, which is just one type "feeding" that is required by the child.

Infants need emotional nourishment just as much as physical nutrients. The nourishment comes through a combination of the above described sensory channels. Whether breast or bottle-fed, the primal gaze, cooing sounds, and gentle snuggling involved with nursing an infant are all critical to nurturing, trust, and a sense of safety.

Due to having a Parent ego state that was programmed by our parents, we tend to care for ourselves in the same way that they cared for us – i.e., our self-care habits today are a product of the nurturing we received back then.

Erikson also identified virtues that develop according to the outcomes of each stage ... for this child development stage the virtue is Hope. With poor outcomes, it becomes more difficult to hope and frequent feelings of hopelessness occur.

1:1 Stage One Self-Assessment:
Unmet needs in each child development stage can be observed in present-day symptoms. For each of the following statements assign a rank between 10 (high) and 0 (not at all).

___ I do not feel I have a right to ask others to meet my needs

___ Feeling close to others frightens me

___ The world feels like an unsafe and fearful place

___ I have a strong need to be in control in order to feel safe

___ I don't like affectionate touch or touching others (hugs, kisses)

___ I have a hard time acknowledging and responding to my own wants and needs

___ I have a difficult time giving attention to others

___ I have a strong or excessive need to be admired by others

___ Despite what others say, I doubt that I'm lovable

___ I have experienced addictions or compulsions involving the mouth (oral, ingestive objects such as drugs, alcohol, food, cigars, cigarettes, chewing tobacco, nail-biting, thumb/finger sucking, etc.)

___ I have difficulty trusting others even if they are trustworthy

___ I lack trust in myself to take care of my needs

___ I do not trust others to care about or respond to my needs

___ I have a tendency to lose hope or feel hopeless about ever being happy or getting what I really want.

___ I have a tendency to trust too early in a relationship or friendship

___ I have deep fears of intimacy because it could result in abandonment

1:2 Journaling Exercise:

Take a few moments to think about each question. Remember that your problems from infancy relate to the need for trust, safety, and nurturance. You may be surprised when you actually start looking here to see the degree of dysfunction that relates back to a specific time in your life. You may feel grateful to have made this discovery, or it may trigger painful feelings.

1.   When was the last time you were held and cuddled by someone you really cared about?

2.   What does trust mean to you?

3.   Are you a trustworthy person? If so, how do you demonstrate trustworthiness?

4.   For whom do you feel the most trust? What is it about this relationship that inspires trust?

5.   Do you generally feel physically and emotionally safe with those for whom you care deeply? How do you feel about this?

6.   How do you feel about being depended on and being dependent upon someone else? Write about those relationships in your life where this is the case.

7.   Do you feel a right to have needs? Are you afraid to acknowledge that you need?

8.   Do you feel your needs are adequately met, or do you feel your needs are mostly unfulfilled? Give details.

9.   Now, explore and combine all the data that you obtained from the developmental questionnaire and the above journal questions to make a list of issues your infant self carries. Some examples are:
   - Inability to trust others to care about or be there for me
   - Inability to feel safe with people or in the world
   - Difficulty knowing what I need and how I feel
   - Inability to trust myself to take care of myself or meet my own needs
   - Difficulty being close to others and telling them how I feel

1:3 Diagram of Possible Outcomes for Stage One:
   The vertical axis on the diagram below represents the range of possible outcomes for Stage One – Healthy Trust (top) to Mistrust (bottom). The horizontal continuum represents the range of possible negative outcomes from frequently Externalizer to frequently Internalizer. Put an "X" anywhere on the diagram that fits with your position in your most intimate present day relationships (most of the time).

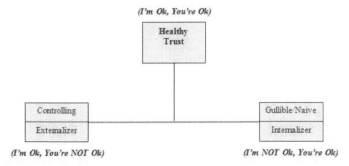

Figure 16: Stage One Outcomes Continuum

Keep in mind that we can move around on this line depending upon the situation, circumstances, and especially what ego-state we are in (Angry Child, Vulnerable Child, Critical Parent, etc.) We are likely to stay in the Adult Ego-State at work or out in public.

In our private lives, especially if we are wounded, with loved ones and family members we cannot avoid being triggered into the Externalization of the Angry/Defiant Child and/or the Internalization of the Vulnerable/Needy Child ego-state. This is where and how the Drama Triangle, Figure-Eight, and other dysfunctional relationship patterns arise. (See THAW, Chapter 7.)

"Internalizers" or Codependents:
People who have disowned or cut themselves off (dissociated) from their Angry/Defiant Child ego-state tend to get caught up in the Internalizer role – such as those who were not allowed to express anger outwardly or perhaps a parent was abusive and a rage-a-holic so that it was dangerous to express your anger.

"Externalizers" or Counter-Dependents:
Those who have disowned or cut themselves off (dissociated) from their Vulnerable Child ego-state tend to gravitate toward the Externalizer position – such as those who were not allowed to have their feelings or families where vulnerable feelings were considered "weak."

Healthy, Positive Outcomes:

Those who had a predominantly positive outcome to this and all other stages are able to own and experience both their Angry/Defiant Child and their Vulnerable/Needy Child ego-states from an integrated position – i.e., because they have not been emotionally wounded, these two essential elements of self are simultaneously active and working together in harmony.

The Normal Function of the Vulnerable/Needy and Angry/Defiant Parts of Self:

A healthy Angry/Defiant part provides access to just enough personal power to establish a sense of separateness while a healthy Vulnerable/Needy part helps let the walls down enough to really connect with others (only those who are safe and also able to connect in healthy ways). It is NOT having the ego-states (i.e., parts of self) that are the problem – it is the level of woundedness that each of the parts carry that causes the reactivity.

Trust, Safety, and Nurturing are the themes during this stage.

The extent to which we have a positive outcome directly influences our abilities to trust, care for, and protect ourselves and others. If we have a negative outcome to this stage we will recycle through the negative emotional themes (abandonment, shame, and contempt) and recreate the experiences of this time in our development until we "get it right" – which is the goal of this section of the program.

Journal Assignments:

Think about how the above fits with you and those closest to you. Write about your thoughts, feelings, and observations in your journal.

[Audio Alert] *Listen to Audio Program 11a – Adult Relationship Timeline*: Listen to the audio and write about trust, safety and nurturing self and other issues you encountered on your adult relationship timeline in your journal.

[Audio Alert] *Listen to Audio Program 11b – Childhood Relationship Timelines:* Listen to the audio and write about trust, safety and nurturing self and other issues you encountered on your childhood relationship timeline in your journal.

1:4 Detecting Your Inner Critic:

[Audio Alert] *Listen to Audio Program 12a – Inner Critic*

This exercise helps to give a form to the critical voice or voices you hear inside your head, so that your Ideal Adult/Parent ego-state can interview, negotiate with, challenge or even confront the negativity. The critical voice for the infant may be the voice that shamed or humiliated you for having needs, for being afraid to trust, for not feeling safe enough to care. These are usually the parental tapes that are recorded inside our unconscious mind. However, many times other sources, such as people at church, school, or in the extended family, may also have had an influence. This could include authority figures as well as peers.

The part of us that carries these shaming messages from the past is our Critical Parent ego-state. We all need this part of us that can take a critical position in order to anticipate obstacles and help us avoid needless problems – but we don't need the shaming, the discounting, and the abusive tones and messages that came from those other sources. Since the infant is preverbal, these "voices" can be more like a feeling than an actual voice at the time the child internalized the messages. As an adult, these feelings gathered in infancy can get translated into "audio tapes."

These voices can be very poisonous or toxic, and can take on many shapes and forms. Their messages are usually very easy to hear, and can be very damaging to your Children within. When working with these critical voices, get support from Higher Power and Protector if needed. Most of your Inner Children will have a specific voice that haunts them from which they will need to be protected.

Journal Assignment:

As you answer the following questions you may want to imagine yourself surrounded by a protective, spiritual light from your Higher Power … don't be surprised if your Child Self answers differently than your adult self.

1. What critical statements do you make to yourself about your ability to care for self (know and meet your needs) and/or your ability to care for significant others (know and meet the needs of those you love)?

2. What critical statements do you make to yourself about your lovability?

3. What critical statements do you make to yourself about your capacity to trust yourself? Other People? The world in general?

4. What critical statements do you make yourself about your trustworthiness and/or the trustworthiness of others?

5. Where have you heard those statements before? Whose voice is this? Is it the voice of a parent? A relative? A teacher? A clergy member? Classmates? Coach? Are these statements that you have heard from society or through the media? Is this voice imagined or real?

6. Imagine that you, as the Inner Adult, speak to this voice. Ask this voice what it wants. What is its positive intention? Is it trying to hurt you, help you … or both?

Remember that all parts-of-self have a positive intention for us, even if they don't produce that outcome. (If it is the voice of an abuser the intention is not usually positive.)

7.   Using your least dominant hand let your Inner Child draw a picture of this critical voice. Keep in mind that to this part of you the picture represents fears, terror, and judgments and may appear as a scary or threatening image such as a "monster" or other typical childhood fear.

[Audio Alert] Listen to Audio Program 12b – Inner Critic 2

When you have finished the picture (above), listen to audio 12b, then go back to the original critical statements in items 1 through 6 above and rewrite them below. Then, next to each critical statement, write a positive affirmation. Notice your self-talk and formulate your affirmation as a response; i.e., if the self-talk uses first-person, then form the affirmation as a response in second-person. (See Examples.)

Examples:
Critical Statement: *I'm so terrible I do not deserve to be loved by anyone.*
Positive Affirmation: *You are lovable just the way you are.*

Critical Statement: *You're so stupid!*
Positive Affirmation: *I'm a bright and competent person.*

NOTE: Remember to have your Ideal Adult/Parent or your Higher Power, interact with this Inner Critic whenever it appears. Have them to use these affirmations whenever you hear these wounding words. Reassure your Inner Child that the critical voice will no longer go unchallenged.

1:5 Stage One: Issues and Symptoms

It's time to consolidate. Review your answers from the Self-Assessment Questionnaire, Audio Programs, your observations about the Outcomes Diagram and journal entries for this stage of development. Now, complete the following Stage One Inner Child Profile below.

It is important to take your time to complete this exercise as thoroughly as possible. Listen to the audio programs as many times as you find helpful or if you get stuck. Don't worry if you cannot find the root cause (i.e., original circumstances), but it is a big bonus if you do. You are likely to uncover even more information in later exercises that will help fill in the blanks. When that happens, just come back here and add anything else that comes up. Here is an example of the Issues and a format to write it out in your journal. Outline as many issues as you can come up with. You cannot over-do this work, but you can under-do it.

- **Identified Issue:** (Problematic behavior)
  I do not trust that others will respond to my needs.
- **The Root Cause:** (Original Circumstances)
  My father was in a bad car accident three months after I was born. I often was left with a babysitter while my mother was at the hospital. When she was at home, her attention was focused on the survival needs of the family, not on the basic needs I had as an infant.
- **Evidence in Present Day:** (How I treat myself) I focus on my work and my relationship with others and often ignore the basic needs of my body.

[Audio Alert] Listen to Audio Program 13a – Reclaim this Child

Your Infant Self may carry pain, but it also carries joy, wonder, and a sense of newness. You may now have a better awareness of these. In the exercises you have done so far, what have you learned about your Infant Self and about how you continue to carry these traits? Write about any thoughts or feelings this question, and audio 13a has provoked.

[Audio Alert] Listen to Audio Program 13b – Adult Meets Child

These meetings with your Inner Children can be emotional; sometimes it's like meeting a stranger, other times it's like meeting an old friend. Record your thoughts, feelings, and reactions to this audio below. End the experience by asking your Infant Self to help you find a photograph or a picture from a magazine that looks like him or her. Paste or tape this picture into your journal so you can look at it and began to ask more in-depth questions and then write about how this picture makes you feel.

1:6 Communication and Daily Dialogue

The exercise will help the Adult-Self separate further from your Children within by helping you determine their likes and their dislikes. It also gives your Child Sself a chance to ask you questions. In this way, the Adult and Child begin to develop a healing and healthy relationship. Here you go inside and imagine having a conversation with your Child within. Record the conversation in your journal. This can become a "daily dialogue" if you choose.

Infants can communicate, but they cannot use words. If you do not get verbal answers from your Child within, try to interpret body language, feelings, sounds, or other sensations that you can intuit. Some people feel they communicate best with this part of themselves using a form of imaginary telepathy. If that works for you, use it. As you work with the older children within, their ability to communicate will mature.

Journal Exercise:

To begin your dialogue, write each question in your journal using your most dominant hand. Use your least dominant hand to record your Inner Children's responses. Use the name for the Child that you chose in the previous visualization exercise.

1. What is your Infant's favorite color? Favorite story? A favorite lullaby?

2. Using your Infant's eyes, look around the room you are in. What is the object in that room your Inner Infant most wants to touch? If it is safe, imagine the Child touches it.

3. What does this Child need the most from you?

4. How does this child feel about you? Does it feel abandoned or ignored by you? Why?

5. Does the Infant understand what it means to be reclaimed by you? If not, explain that it means he/she will longer be alone again; you will make sure that the basic needs are met.

6. Does your baby like to be held? If so, imagine a rocking chair and sit with the Infant for a while. Write about this experience.

7. Is there anything the Infant wants to know about you?

8. What joys does this Child want to offer you and what prevents this from happening?

Learn to use this journal exercise daily by tuning into the feelings you have throughout the day and realizing that it may be one of your Inner Children signaling you that they need your attention. Remember the format for "feelings as signals from your Inner Child" to know when the Child needs to talk with you.

1:7 Developing a Protector
Each Inner Child may want to have its own Protector, sometimes more than one. Start by letting your Child within

first create the one that it needs the most. This Protector is the character you bring in to provide special care that the Adult Self is unable to provide.

Creating a Protector is a way to ensure that your Inner Child will never be alone. It's as if this Protector is assigned to your Inner Child and will always be there to care, even when your Adult Self is occupied in your day-to-day affairs. There are no guidelines for creating this Protector, let your Inner Children be your guide.

Journal Exercise:

1. Ask the Child within to tell you about the person or character for which it feels the most trust. If your Child can select anyone in the world, real or imagined, to always be there, who would it choose? (It can be Superman, an angel, Mother Teresa, or your Higher Power. It can also be a relative, movie star, or a childhood friend's parent.)

2. Ask your Inner Child to draw a picture that represents this Protector. Have the Child use crayons or colored pencils and use the least dominant hand to draw the picture.

3. Assure your Inner Child that this Protector will be available any time the Child needs that Protector.

Keep this picture in your journal and keep it stored in your imagination, too. Always be ready to call in this Protector for support in your work with your Inner Child. This character will care for, protect, and entertain your Child. It is this image that will help meet the emotional needs of your Child and heal the gaps left from the Child.

Complete this exercise by making a partnership between this Protector and the Adult-Self. Call in your Higher Power as well, if this seems appropriate, because these three make up the team that will heal the Children within. Record any thoughts, feelings, or other reactions to this exercise in your journal.

1:8 Grieving your Losses

This exercise will take you step-by-step through the grieving process so that you may let go of the blocked emotions from this stage of your development. You have gathered a lot of information from the previous exercises. Don't worry if you don't feel you have many answers to the following questions in this stage. Trust your instinct, let the answers come to you intuitively, and do the best you can.

Some steps of this process are done by you as the Adult, and some are done by you as the Inner Child. Remember to use your least dominant hand when responding from the Child and your dominant hand when responding from the Adult. This will help you more easily switch back and forth between these two parts of yourself.

Journal Exercises:

You will need your journal, drawing materials, and separate sheets of paper. *Do these exercises* on the *loose sheets of paper* – not in your journal. Everyone grieves in his own way. If any section of these exercises does not seem right for you, just discard or change that section and complete the ones that do seem to fit.

1. In your mind's-eye, see your Infant Child in front of you. Ask that part of you to consider times/events in the past when you felt panic, hurt, sadness, or fear about safety, nurturing, and/or trust. List these events one-by-one and then prioritize them from least painful to most painful. For our purposes here, don't worry about describing the events or experiences in detail … just give them a name such as "that time in the kitchen with so-and-so." If the experience is too painful, just use one or two words to describe it for now such as "kitchen."

2. Now ask your Inner Child to draw a picture representing the feelings he or she has carried over the years (artistic talent not required). Have the Child draw one picture for each of the events or experiences you just listed above from least painful to most painful. Then, reflect on any other times in your life when you felt panic, hurt, or fear about safety, nurturing, and/or trust issues ... draw a picture for any of these times you feel would be appropriate (no more than ten examples).

3. Now, as your Adult Self, think back to the times you've tried to control these situations in your life so you wouldn't have to feel these feelings. Then list the survival skills your Little Professor devised to try to manipulate, bargain, or control in an attempt to get this Child's needs for safety, nurturing, or trust met at those times (e.g., people pleasing, approval seeking, victim stance, angry outbursts, distancing or pursuing, clinging or pushing away, addictions, etc.).

4. Now, as your Adult Self, write a letter explaining to your Child Self that it was not his/her fault that their needs were unmet and, in your own words, tell the Child that the problems in the family were not caused by him/her either. Furthermore, describe to your Child the way it should have been and anything you know about why it was not that way. Be supportive, encouraging, and give the Child permission to break the "Don't Talk, Don't Feel, Don't Trust" rules. Let this part of you know it is okay to have your feelings now because you are here to protect and allow that.

5. Now, help your Child write a letter to your parents expressing any anger, sadness, grief and other feelings that your Child has held over the years. As you finish the letter, let any feelings surface and come out as you comfort your Inner Child. (You might want to use a teddy bear and rocking chair combined with the

sanctuary or other safe place of your own choosing to facilitate this experience.)

6.   When you feel ready to continue, as the healthy Adult you, write a letter to your Child-Self stating how you feel about the care he or she received. Tell your Child within what you're willing to provide for him or her from this time forward. Imagine your Adult-Self reading this letter to your Inner Child somewhere, one-on-one in the sanctuary. Again, as you complete this, imagine that you comfort your Child-Self in whatever way seems best to you.

7.   Conclude this grieving process by closing your eyes and surround yourself and your Inner Child with spiritual light from your Higher Power. In the next step, all the pain that has been expressed will be released and all the wounds that have been opened will be healed. Take a cleansing breath and bring your focus back to the room and open your eyes.

1:9 Releasing Blocked Emotions

This exercise lets your Inner Child release the pain in two ways: emotionally, and spiritually. For the process of emotional release, you will need the following items: your journal, all your drawings and writings from the previous step, a copy of the picture of your Inner Child, and a campfire (outside) or fireplace (inside). If inside, scented candles, background music (CD) and a comfortable, safe space where you won't be interrupted are also suggested.

Again, if any section of these exercises does not seem right for you, just discard or modify that section and complete the ones that do seem to fit.

Emotional Release…

1.   Set up your space, light your candles if you choose, and put on your music. Now, take all the drawings,

writings, and letters that you prepared in the previous steps and decide which ones you feel you need to release in the fire. Also, have your picture of this Child nearby.

2.   Imagine the light within your body begins to grow and expand until it surrounds you and fills up the entire room/area. Now, in your mind's-eye, bring in your Child-Self … hold him or her safely in your arms, or comfortably settle your Infant Child somewhere in the room/area. You may want to use a teddy bear to symbolize the younger Children within.

3.   Focus on the feelings you will be releasing. Mentally review the work you and your Child have done, the issues you have discovered, and the healing you have experienced so far. Now, silently ask your Child if he or she is ready to let go of the pain.

4.   When the two of you are ready, take one of the drawings, letters, or pieces of writing and symbolically release it by dropping it into the fire. Imagine the emotions represented on that piece of paper are released into the flame and carried away by the smoke. Release your Inner Child's drawing that represents the panic and fear, your list of bargaining behaviors, the anger, despair and any other letters or written work you feel a need to release. Burn one piece of paper at a time, so you're able to focus on the contents of that page.

1:10 Release and Reimprinting this Stage

[Audio Alert] Listen to Audio Program 14a – Spiritual Release

Now record this experience in your journal. This Child has much joy and comfort to offer you once the trust is there that you will meet his or her needs. Know that if the pain of this younger self gets triggered that you will be able to separate from the pain by letting the Child remain safely in the Sanctuary while the Adult you attends to the triggering situation.

Your fears of being loved and your caution about trusting others will never completely disappear. In fact, it would not even be desirable to have them gone. It is important to be able to determine when it is safe and appropriate to trust as well as when it is not. Just know that, by completing this work the wounds of abandonment have been treated and a healing process initiated. You will get better and better, every day in every way!

[Audio Alert] Listen to Audio Program 14b – Parental Timeline Reimprinting

Listen to the audio at least two times or more. Really allow the ideas and images to become vivid and know that you are giving yourself more options by doing so. Write about your experience of the audio in your journal.

[Bonus Audio] Return to Audio #1: Majestic Meadow

As an extra benefit you may complete this work with your Inner Infant by returning to Majestic Meadow and the garden of your thoughts. Ask your Inner Infant how it would like to contribute to this garden now. It may choose certain plants or flowers to symbolically represent a new perspective, healing, and/or the gifts it can now bring to your experiences. Imagine that the two of you make these contributions together so that this Inner Child will be represented in the garden of your growth.

Stage Two - Autonomy vs. Shame and Doubt
Toddler (2-4 years old)

This developmental stage is where we begin to form a separate sense of self and also influences our initial attitudes and abilities regarding boundary-setting, independence, curiosity, imagination, and willingness to explore.

In stage two the child experiences the initial development of a "mind of its own" often referred to as the will. This is the child's first real attempt to pull away and separate from mother; the reward is a sense of autonomy.

Just as infancy involves a healthy co-dependence, entrance into the toddler and pre-school stages of child development marks the beginning of a healthy counter-dependence. Well-known as the "terrible twos," this is the time when the child discovers the abilities to say no and to use anger as a means of getting what it wants.

Also known as the "second birth," or the emotional birth, this stage gives us the first glimpses of the Angry/Defiant Child ego-state, although its official debut is not until the onset of adolescence. Allowing and even encouraging this bid for independence while maintaining a good balance with parental authority is the major factor in the outcome of this stage. Knowing when to let them win and choosing your battles wisely are two parenting skills that will come in handy.

There is also a strong feeling of ambivalence in this stage – the toddler does not tolerate mother being out of sight for long, yet they desire more independence. As they move further away they will often turn around to make sure mom is still there.

If a parent does not allow any exploration of the limits in an accepting and non-judgmental way the child begins to develop a sense of shame due to their frustrated need to separate. They then begin to experience excessive self-doubt, which is present to some degree anyway. Eventually, they can give up trying to gain autonomy and remain needy. This can provide reassurance to the parent that needs to be needed, and she can foster more of the same.

On the other hand, if they are given blanket approval for everything they do the child can develop what's often referred to as "spoiled child syndrome." Later these kids really have trouble hearing and accepting the word "No." In all stages of child development children are natural-born limit-testers. They will push ... and push ... and push the limits until someone steps in and says "No."

Just as they will seek approval and attention, kids seek discipline when there is not enough of it. If they don't get healthy discipline, they can develop a false sense of entitlement. Many veteran parents can relate to a time when they have firmly said "No" and re-enforced it with a time-out or other form of discipline. When this happens the toddler seems to change quickly from angry and defiant to warm and cuddly as if some need has been satisfied – because it has.

When children don't know where the limits are they can begin to feel unsafe. Testing the limits and experiencing the appropriate reaction of their parents, they can feel safe again – as if at some level they get the message "when I can't stop myself, someone will be there to stop me."

2: 1 Stage Two Self-Assessment

Unmet needs in each child development stage can be observed in present-day symptoms. For each of the following statements assign a rank between 10 (high) and 0 (not at all).

___ I find it difficult to say no to people.

___ When I do say no, I say it abruptly or stubbornly because I fear their rejection.

___ I do not say no to those I am close to because I think they won't like me.

___ I do not say no to my significant other because I am afraid they will go away and not come back.

___ When making plans with friends, I tend to agree with whatever they say or suggest.

___ If I ask someone to do something for me and am told no, I feel shame that I even asked.

___ I am afraid to assert myself at work. I may get fired or my boss might say no.

___ If my partner, family member, or friend is angry, I assume I have done something wrong.

___ I feel embarrassed if I'm with someone who makes a scene in public. I assume others will think less of me.

___ I feel smothered if someone gets too close.

___ If a friend calls and is feeling low, I feel inadequate if I cannot do something to cheer my friend up.

___ I don't say anything if my partner, family member, or friend uses something of mine that I don't want them to use.

___ If a friend from out-of-town calls and wants to stay at my house, I say yes, even if it's inconvenient for me.

___ If I need a quiet evening at home and a friend calls in need of company, I will still agree to get together.

___ If my boss asks me to work late, I say yes, even if I have other plans.

___ If I asked someone to do something for me, and they tell me no, I feel resentful.

___ I get very angry when I don't get my way

2:2 Journaling Exercise:

What do your answers reveal to you about your comfort level with boundaries and setting limits? If you scored six or above on any item, those are the issues of your Toddler Self you will want to address.

1. Think of two or three recent occasions when you wanted to say no, but did not. Describe the situation and write about how that feels.

2. Think of two or three recent times when someone said no to you. How did you feel? Describe the situation.

3. What feelings get triggered when you're around someone who is emotionally upset? How do you respond? Do you feel overly responsible for their feelings? If so, how?

4. Think about the people with whom you spend the most time. How do you feel after you've seen them? If that person is depressed, do you feel depressed? If that person is exhilarated, do you feel exhilarated? What does that say about your emotional enmeshment with this other person? (Enmeshment means "tangled up or entanglement.") Did this happen to you as a child with your parent or caretaker?

5. Are you more comfortable being close or do you feel more secure being distant? If "that depends" explain the both conditions.

6. In romantic relationships, do you become preoccupied with your partner's needs and tend to lose sight of your own? If so, list examples of this behavior and write down your thoughts about this.

7. Now, explore and combine all the data that you obtained from the developmental questionnaire and these journal questions to make a list of issues your toddler self carries. **Some examples are:**

- Inability to say no to friends because you are afraid they will reject you
- Inability to set limits with your boss because you fear you might get fired
- Difficulty stating how you feel because you fear you will be humiliated or rejected
- Feeling smothered if someone tries to get too close
- Feeling inadequate if a friend is upset, and you cannot make that friend feel better

2:3 Diagram of Possible Outcomes for Stage Two:

The vertical axis on the diagram below represents the range of possible outcomes for Stage One – Healthy Boundaries (top) to Toxic Shame (bottom). The horizontal continuum represents the range of possible negative outcomes from frequently Externalizer to frequently Internalizer. Put an "X" anywhere on the diagram that fits with your position in your most intimate present day relationships (most of the time).

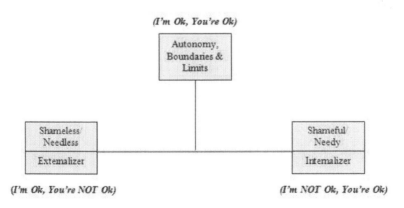

Figure 17: Stage Two Outcomes Continuum

Keep in mind that we can move around on this line depending upon the situation, circumstances, and especially what ego-state we are in (Angry Child, Vulnerable Child, Critical Parent, etc.) We are likely to stay in the Adult Ego-State at work or out in public.

In our private lives, especially if we are wounded, with loved ones and family members we cannot avoid being triggered into the Externalization of the Angry/Defiant Child and/or the Internalization of the Vulnerable/Needy Child ego-state. This is where and how the Drama Triangle, Figure-Eight, and other dysfunctional relationship patterns arise. (See THAW, Chapter 7)

"Internalizers" or Codependents:

People who have disowned or cut themselves off (dissociated) from their Angry/Defiant Child ego-state tend to get caught up in the Internalizer role – such as those who were not allowed to express anger outwardly or perhaps a parent was abusive and a rage-a-holic so that it was dangerous to express your anger.

"Externalizers" or Counter-Dependents:

Those who have disowned or cut themselves off (dissociated) from their Vulnerable Child ego-state tend to gravitate toward the Externalizer position – such as those who were not allowed to have their feelings or families where vulnerable feelings were considered "weak."

Healthy, Positive Outcomes:

Those who had a predominantly positive outcome to this and all other stages are able to own and experience both their Angry/Defiant Child and their Vulnerable/Needy Child ego-states from an integrated position – i.e., because they have not been emotionally wounded, these two essential elements of self are simultaneously active and working together in harmony.

The Normal Function of the Vulnerable/Needy and Angry/Defiant Parts of Self:

A healthy Angry/Defiant Part provides access to just enough personal power to establish a sense of separateness while a healthy Vulnerable/Needy part helps let the walls down enough to really connect with others (only those who are safe and also able to connect in healthy ways). It is NOT having the ego-states (i.e., parts of self) that are the problem – it is the level of original pain that each of the parts carry that causes the reactivity.

A solid sense of self, knowing your limits, setting healthy boundaries, and your ability to say AND hear the word "no," are the themes during this stage.

The extent to which we have a positive outcome directly influences our abilities to trust, care for, and protect ourselves and others. If we have a negative outcome to this stage we will recycle through the negative emotional themes (abandonment, shame, and contempt) and recreate the experiences of this time in our development until we "get it right" – which is the goal of this section of the program.

Journal Assignment:

Think about how this diagram and issues fit with you and those closest to you. Which outcomes did each of your parents demonstrate most often? How about your past and present relationships? Which outcomes did you and your partners tend to demonstrate? Do you see any patterns or other interesting observations? Note your thoughts and observations in your journal.

[Audio Alert] Listen to Audio Program 21a – Relationship Timelines

Journal Assignment: Write about issues regarding your ability to maintain a solid sense of self, knowing your limits, setting healthy boundaries, and your ability to say AND hear the word "no" that you encountered on your adult relationship timeline.

[Audio Alert] Listen to Audio Program 21b – Relationship Timelines

Journal Assignment: Write about issues regarding your ability to maintain a solid sense of self, knowing your limits, setting healthy boundaries, and the ability to say AND hear the word "no" that you encountered on your childhood relationship timeline.

2:4 Detecting Your Inner Critic:

[Audio Alert] Listen to Audio Program 22a – Inner Critic

This exercise helps to give a form to the critical voice or voices you hear inside your head, so that your Ideal Adult/Parent ego-state can communicate with, challenge or confront the negativity. The critical voice for the Toddler Self may ridicule you for saying no, shame you when someone says no to you, and convinces you that you have no right to be autonomous and independent. It may be a voice that suggests that you ignore other people's boundaries and disregard them when they say no.

The part of us that carries these shaming messages from the past is our Critical Parent ego-state. We all need this part of us that can take a critical position in order to anticipate obstacles and help us avoid needless problems – but we don't need the shaming, the discounting, and the abusive tones and messages that came from those other sources. Since the Toddler borders on pre-verbal, these "voices" may be more like a feeling than an actual voice at the time the child internalized the messages. As an adult, these feelings gathered in early childhood can get translated into "audio tapes."

These voices can be very poisonous or toxic, and can take on many shapes and forms. Its messages are usually very easy to hear, and can be very damaging to your Children within. When working with these critical voices, get support from Higher Power and Protector if needed. Most of your Inner

Children will have a specific voice that haunts them from which they will need to be protected.

As you answer the following questions you may want to imagine yourself surrounded by a protective, spiritual light from your Higher Power don't be surprised if your Child Self answers differently than you the adult:

1.   What critical statements do you make to yourself when you say or hear the word "no?"

2.   What critical statements do you make yourself when you set boundaries or attempt to be independent in a relationship?

3.   What critical statements do you make to yourself when you catch yourself acting spontaneous and self-confident?

4.   What critical statements do you make to yourself when you want to stop feeling engulfed (swallowed-up) or rejected by someone you like?

5.   Where have you heard those statements before? Whose voice is this? Is it the voice of a parent? A relative? A teacher? A clergy member? Classmate? Coach? Are these statements that you have heard from society or through the media? Is this voice imagined or real?

6.   Imagine that you, as the Inner Adult, speak to this voice. Ask this voice what it wants. What is its positive intention? Is it trying to hurt you, help you … or both? Remember that all parts of self have a positive intention for us even if they don't produce that outcome. (If it is the voice of an abuser the intention is not usually positive.)

7.   Using your least dominant hand let your Inner Child draw a picture of this critical voice. Keep in mind that to this part of you the picture represents fears, terror, and judgments and may appear as a scary or threatening image such as a "monster" or other typical childhood fear.

When you have finished the picture, go back to the original critical statements in items 1 through 6 above and rewrite them in your journal. Then, next to each critical statement, write a positive affirmation. Notice your self-talk and formulate your affirmation as a response; i.e., if the self-talk uses first-person, then form the affirmation as a response in second-person. (See Examples.)

[Audio Alert] Listen to Audio Program 22b – Inner Critic 2

Examples:

Critical Statement: *If I say no then he/she may leave me.*
Positive Affirmation: *When you set limits you strengthen the relationship.*

Critical Statement: *You're so selfish!*
Positive Affirmation: *It's my right and responsibility to take care of my needs.*

NOTE:
Remember to have your Ideal Adult/Parent or your Higher Power interact with this Inner Critic whenever it appears. Have them to use these affirmations whenever you hear these wounding words. Reassure your Inner Child that the critical voice will no longer go unchallenged.

2:5 Stage Two, Issues and Symptoms

Review your answers from the Self-Assessment Questionnaire, Audio Programs, your observations about the Outcomes Diagram and journal entries for this stage of development. Now, complete the following Stage Two Inner Child Profile below.

It is important to take your time to fill out this worksheet thoroughly as possible. Listen to the audio programs as many times as you find helpful or if you get stuck. Don't worry if you cannot find the catalyst (i.e., original circumstances), but it is a big bonus if you do. You are likely to uncover even more information in later exercises that will help fill in the blanks. When that happens, just come back here and add anything else that comes up.

2:5 Stage Two: Issues and Symptoms

It's time to consolidate. Review your answers from the Self-Assessment Questionnaire, Audio Programs, your observations about the Outcomes Diagram and journal entries for this stage of development. Now, complete the following Stage Two Inner Child Profile below.

It is important to take your time to complete this exercise as thoroughly as possible. Listen to the audio programs as many times as you find helpful or if you get stuck. Don't worry if you cannot find the root cause (i.e., original circumstances), but it is a big bonus if you do. You are likely to uncover even more information in later exercises that will help fill in the blanks. When that happens, just come back here and add anything else that comes up. Here is an example of the Issues and a format to write it out in your journal. Outline as many issues as you can come up with. You cannot over-do this work, but you can under-do it.

- **Identified Issue:** (Problematic behavior)
  I have trouble saying no to those closest to me because I am afraid if I do, they will get mad and leave me.

- **The Root Cause:** (Original Circumstances)
  My father did this. He was very strict. "Talking back" was not allowed. If we said no, we were sent to our rooms for the night and he refused to talk to us for several days.
- **Evidence in Present Day:** (How I treat myself)
  I have been unable to stay on a diet and say no to any food that is offered to me by another. I feel disgusted with myself and get depressed.

[Audio Alert] Listen to Audio Program 23a – Reclaim this Child

Your Toddler Self may carry pain, but it also carries curiosity, independence, and a sense of adventure. You may now have a better awareness of these. In the exercises you have done so far, what have you learned about your Toddler Self and about how you continue to carry these traits? Write about any thoughts or feelings this question, and audio 23a, has provoked.

[Audio Alert] Listen to Audio Program 23b – Adult Meets Child

These meetings with your Inner Children can be emotional; sometimes it's like meeting a stranger, other times it's like meeting an old friend. Record your thoughts, feelings, and reactions to this audio below. End the experience by asking your Toddler Self to help you find a photograph or a picture from a magazine that looks like him or her. Paste or tape this picture into your journal so you can look at it and began to ask more in-depth questions and then write about how this picture makes you feel.

2:6 Communication and Daily Dialogue

The exercise will help the Adult-Self separate further from your Children within by helping you determine their likes and their dislikes. It also gives your Child self a chance to ask you questions. In this way, the Adult and Child begin to develop a healing and healthy relationship. Here you go inside and imagine having a conversation with your Child within. Record the conversation in your journal. This can become a "daily dialogue" if you choose.

If you do not get verbal answers from your Child within, try to interpret body language, feelings, sounds, or other sensations that you can intuit. Some people feel they communicate best with this part of themselves using a form of imaginary telepathy. If that works for you, use it. As you work with the older Children within, their ability to communicate will mature.

To begin your dialogue, write each question in your journal using your most dominant hand. Use your least dominant hand to record your Inner Children's responses. Use the name for the Child that you chose in the previous visualization exercise.

1. Does your Toddler Child have a favorite bedtime story? A favorite toy? A favorite play place? Ask the Child to show them to you.

2. What activity does your Toddler most enjoy?

3. Ask your Toddler to tell you about his or her fear of being left because of misbehavior or fear of hearing the word "no." These feelings may have been experienced back in the Child's day or the Child may experience these fears in present day relationships.

4. How does this Child feel about you? Does it feel abandoned or ignored by you? Why?

5. Does the Toddler understand what it means to be reclaimed by you? If not, explain that it means you will listen to this part of self when it feels a boundary has been crossed, and it needs you to set a limit.

6. What does this Child need the most from you?

7. Does your Toddler within feel comfortable with your setting of limits and saying "no."

8. Ask your Toddler Self if you parent him/her in a similar way as your parents did. If so, how does this feel?

9. Is there anything the Toddler wants to know about you? Does it trust you to protect its boundaries and respond to its needs?

Learn to use this journal exercise daily by tuning into the feelings you have throughout the day and realizing that it may be one of your Inner Children signaling you that they need your attention. Remember the format for "feelings as signals from your Inner Child" to know when the Child needs to talk with you.

2:7 Developing a Protector

Each Inner Child may want to have its own Protector, sometimes more than one. Start by letting your Child within first create the one that it needs the most. This Protector is the character you bring in to provide special care that the Adult self is unable to provide.

Creating a Protector is a way to ensure that your Inner Child will never be alone. It's as if this Protector is assigned to your Inner Child and will always be there to care, even when your Adult self is occupied in your day-to-day affairs. There are no guidelines for creating this Protector, let your Inner Children be your guide.

Journal Exercise:

1. Ask the Child within to tell you about the person or character for which it feels the most trust. If your Child can select anyone in the world, real or imagined, to always be there, who would choose? (It can be

Superman, an angel, Mother Teresa, or your Higher Power. It can also be a relative, movie star, or a childhood friend's parent.)

2. Ask your Inner Child to draw a picture that represents this Protector. Have the Child use crayons or colored pencils and use the least dominant hand to draw the picture.

3. Assure your Inner Child that this Protector will be available any time the Child needs that Protector.

Keep this picture in your journal and keep it stored in your imagination, too. Always be ready to call in this Protector for support in your work with your Toddler Child. This character will care for, protect, and entertain your Child. It is this image that will help meet the emotional needs of your Child and heal the gaps left from the Child.

Complete this exercise by making a partnership between this Protector and the Adult-Self. Call in your Higher Power as well, if this seems appropriate, because these three make up the team that will heal the Children within. Record any thoughts, feelings, or other reactions to this exercise in your journal.

2:8 Grieving your Losses

This exercise will take you step-by-step through the grieving process so that you may let go of the blocked emotions from this stage of your development. You have gathered a lot of information from the previous exercises. Don't worry if you don't feel you have many answers to the following questions in this stage. Trust your instinct, let the answers come to you intuitively, and do the best you can.

Some steps of this process are done by you as the Adult, and some are done by you as the Inner Child. Remember to use your least dominant hand when responding from the Child and your dominant hand when responding from the Adult. This will help you more easily switch back and forth between these two parts of yourself.

Journal Exercises:

You will need your journal, drawing materials, and separate sheets of paper. *Do these exercises* on the *loose sheets of paper* – not in your journal. Everyone grieves in his own way. If any section of these exercises does not seem right for you, just discard or change that section and complete the ones that do seem to fit.

1.   In your mind's-eye, see your Toddler Child in front of you. Ask that part of you to consider times/events in the past when you felt panic, hurt, sadness, or fear about setting boundaries, exploring new activities, and taking risks. List these events one by one and then prioritize them from least painful to most painful. For our purposes here, don't worry about describing the events or experiences in detail … just give them a name such as "that time in the kitchen with so-and-so." If the experience is too painful, just use one or two words to describe it for now such as "kitchen."

2.   Now ask your Inner Child to draw a picture representing the feelings he or she has carried over the years (artistic talent not required). Have the Child draw one picture for each of the events or experiences you just listed above from least painful to most painful. Then, reflect on any other times in your life when you felt panic, hurt, or fear about setting boundaries, exploring new activities, and taking risks – draw a picture for any of these times you feel would be appropriate (no more than ten examples).

3.   Now, as your adult self, think back to the times you've tried to control these situations in your life so you wouldn't have to feel these feelings. Then list the

survival skills your Little Professor devised to try to manipulate, bargain, or control in an attempt to get this Child's needs for safety, nurturing, or trust met at those times (e.g., hostility, aggressiveness, persecutor stance, angry outbursts, distancing or pursuing, addictions, etc.).

4. Now, as your Adult Self, write a letter explaining to your Toddler Self that it was not his/her fault that their needs were unmet and, in your own words, tell the Child that the problems in the family were not caused by him/her either. Furthermore, describe to your Child the way it should have been and anything you know about why it was not that way. Be supportive, encouraging, and give the Child permission to break the "Don't Talk, Don't Feel, Don't Trust" rules. Let this part of you know it is okay to have your feelings now because you are here to protect and allow that.

5. Now, help your Toddler write a letter to your parents expressing any anger, sadness, grief and other feelings that your Child has held over the years. As you finish the letter, let any feelings surface and come out as you comfort your Inner Child. (You might want to use a teddy bear and rocking chair combined with the sanctuary or other safe place of your own choosing to facilitate this experience.)

6. When you feel ready to continue, as the healthy Adult you, write a letter to your Toddler-Self stating how you feel about the care he or she received. Tell your Child within what you're willing to provide for him or her from this time forward. Imagine your Adult-Self reading this letter to your Inner Child somewhere, one on one in the sanctuary. Again, as you complete this, imagine that you comfort your Child-Self in whatever way seems best to you.

7. Conclude this grieving process by closing your eyes and surround yourself and your Inner Child with spiritual light from your Higher Power. In the next step, all the pain that has been express will be released in all the wounds that have been opened will be healed. Take a cleansing breath and bring your focus back to the room and open your eyes.

2:9 Releasing Blocked Emotions

This exercise lets your Inner Child release the pain in two ways: emotionally, and spiritually. For the process of emotional release, you will need the following items: your journal, all your drawings and writings from the previous step, a copy of the picture of your Inner Child, and a campfire (outside) or fireplace (inside). If inside, scented candles, background music (CD) and a comfortable, safe space where you won't be interrupted are also suggested.

Again, if any section of these exercises does not seem right for you, just discard or modify that section and complete the ones that do seem to fit.

Emotional Release...

1. Set up your space, light your candles if you choose, and put on your music. Now, take all the drawings, writings, and letters that you prepared in the previous steps and decide which ones you feel you need to release in the fire. Also, have your picture of this Child nearby.

2. Imagine the light within your body begins to grow and expand until it surrounds you and fills up the entire room/area. Now, in your mind's-eye, bring in your Child-Self ... hold him or her safely in your arms, or comfortably settle your Toddler Child somewhere in the room/area. You may want to use a teddy bear to symbolize the younger Children within.

3. Focus on the feelings you will be releasing. Mentally review the work you and your Child have done, the issues you have discovered, and the healing you have experienced so far. Now, silently ask your Child if he or she is ready to let go of the pain.

4. When the two of you are ready, take one of the drawings, letters, or pieces of writing and symbolically release it by dropping it into the fire. Imagine the emotions represented on that piece of paper are released into the flame and carried away by the smoke. Release your Inner Child's drawing that represents the panic and fear, your list of bargaining behaviors, the anger, despair and any other letters or written work you feel a need to release. Burn one piece of paper at a time, so you're able to focus on the contents of that page.

2:10 Release and Reimprinting this Stage

[Audio Alert] Listen to Audio Program 24a – Spiritual Release

Now record this experience in your journal. This Child has much joy and adventure to offer once the trust is there that you will meet his or her needs. Know that if the pain of this younger self gets triggered that you will be able to separate from the pain by letting the Child remain safely in the Sanctuary while the Adult you attends to the triggering situation.

Your fears of setting boundaries and your caution about taking risks may never completely disappear. In fact, it would not even be desirable to have them gone. It is important to be able to determine when it is safe and appropriate to trust as well as when it is not. Just know that, by completing this work the wounds of abandonment have been treated and a healing process initiated. You will get better and better, every day in every way!

[Audio Alert] Listen to Audio Program 24b – Parental Timeline Reimprinting

Listen to the audio at least two times or more. Really allow the ideas and images to become vivid and know that you are giving yourself more options by doing so. Write about your experience of the audio in your journal.

[Bonus Audio] Return to Audio #1: Majestic Meadow

As an extra benefit you may complete this work with your Inner Child by returning to Majestic Meadow and the garden of your thoughts. Ask your Inner Toddler how it would like to contribute to this garden now. It may choose certain plants or flowers to symbolically represent a new perspective, healing, and/or the gifts it can now bring to your experiences. Imagine that the two of you make these contributions together so that this Inner Child will be represented in the garden of your growth.

Stage Three - Initiative vs. Guilt
Pre-Schooler (4-7 years old)

In the Pre-Schooler stage the child begins to take the initiative to explore the world around them and try new things. Their curiosity gets the best of them as they continue to venture out further and further away from mom and dad. During this stage of development children are very impressionable. They need permission and encouragement to explore – always within safe limits of course.

Over-protective or fearful parents can send a message that it is not okay – and, in fact, even dangerous to explore the world. They do this because they "are just making sure that their child doesn't get hurt." Frequent harsh criticism from parents who demand that their children "behave themselves at all times" and "don't get into things" can inhibit their natural curiosity and lead to excessive guilt.

Enough guilt can turn to toxic shame. John Bradshaw explains the difference between guilt and shame this way"; "Guilt says, I MADE a mistake … Toxic Shame says, I AM a mistake." Also, since Stage Three takes place during the imprint period, the lessons learned become deeply ingrained in the neural networks on "how things are done" in life. For example, rigid rules can translate into all-or-nothing functioning later in the life of the child.

Frequent criticism can become a way of seeing self or others. This leads to excessive self-criticism and/or criticism of others – either way an unhealthy existential position that would need to be confirmed over and over again in the child's life. The Critical Parent ego-state comes onto the scene in this stage.

In the case of the over-protective parent, there is an interpersonal transfer of anxiety from parent to child. In the case of the overly rigid and critical parent, it's an interpersonal transfer of shame. In essence, then, the parent subconsciously passes on their own anxiety and or shame to the child. Notice I said "subconsciously." Most parents love their kids and want the best for them. They would never consciously choose to put that burden on their child.

That being said, if we carry these things within as parents, unattended, they will leak out of every pore of our body. And kids in the imprint period are like sponges – they soak up everything. Our non-verbal behavior is a much more powerful teacher than words could ever be for little kids. Most over-protected children who have accumulated anxieties and fears from their parents tend to become passive, indecisive, and timid. Alternatively, they may have a reaction formation and swing into the opposite direction by behaving aggressively and developing an unhealthy fearlessness.

Kids who have been frequently criticized by rigid, controlling parents tend to become Internalizers and take the blame for everything that goes wrong – unless they over-identify with the critical parent in which case, they mimic their behavior becoming an Externalizer, who is over-critical of others.

3:1 Stage Three Self-Assessment

Unmet needs in each child development stage can be observed in present-day symptoms. For each of the following statements assign a rank between 10 (high) and 0 (not at all).

____ I focus on things about myself that I do not like.

____ If I do one thing wrong at work, I obsess about that one thing and discount any other achievements I have made during that day.

____ I spend a great deal of time worrying about what others think of me.

____ My internal dialog is made up of self-critical statements.

____ I am very judgmental of others.

___ I have a hard time accepting or tolerating the imperfections of my friends and coworkers.

___ I dislike people who are too fat or too skinny.

___ If I'm at a party, I feel more secure if I feel that I look better than most of the people there.

___ If something goes wrong at work, I feel responsible even when it couldn't possibly be my fault.

___ If a store clerk is rude to me, I assume I must have done something wrong.

___ I believe it is conceited to say positive things about myself.

___ If a friend says he or she will meet me and is late, I refuse to make plans with that person again.

___ If I make a mistake while participating in a new activity, I never engage in that activity again.

___ If I ask someone to do me a favor and am refused, I never ask again.

___ When I look at my body in the mirror, I focus on what I want to change.

___ I have sex with someone because I do not know any other way to feel close.

___ I have sex because I am angry or sad, and I want to get away from those feelings.

___ I am afraid to relax and let someone else be in command, because I fear something will go wrong, and I will be at fault.

___ It is easier to do a task myself than ask someone else to do it. He or she would not do it the way I want to be done anyway.

___ I feel that if I don't do it, no one will.

___ I'm afraid to ask about something I don't understand because I'm afraid others will think I'm stupid.

___ I dislike it when others ask irrelevant questions

___ I have to understand how to do something immediately, or else I lose interest.

___ I refrain from asking people questions that are too personal.

3:2 Journaling Exercise:

What do your answers reveal to you about your comfort level with boundaries and setting limits? If you scored six or above on any item, those are the issues of your Pre-Schooler Self you will want to address.

1. Think of a recent time when you felt critical of someone else. How did you deal with that feeling? Did you express it, repress it, or deny it? If so, how did you do that?

2. What does your criticism of this other person reveal about you? What emotional reaction did this behavior trigger in you?

3. What do you do when you begin to see these things in other people that you do not like?

4. Define what shame means to you. Think of a time when you felt shame. Describe the incident. Which

elements of this experience triggered those feelings of shame?

5.   What areas of your life are affected by your shame? Does it get in the way of how you relate to your body or the amount of money you make? Does it influence your sexuality, creativity, or intellectual abilities?

6.   Define guilt. Do you experience guilt differently than shame? How?

7.   How do you use sexuality in relationships? Do you focus on sex too much or not enough?

8.   Are you curious; are you comfortable asking questions even if you feel you'll appear stupid?

9.   Now, explore and combine all the data that you obtained from the developmental questionnaire and these journal questions to make a list of issues your Inner Pre-Schooler carries. Some examples are:

   a.   Feeling awkward about your body
   b.   Been highly critical of yourself – full of shame
   c.   Using sex as the only way to feel close
   d.   Being a perfectionist; expecting too much from yourself and others
   e.   Having no tolerance for another person's behavior and/or appearance

3:3 Diagram of Possible Outcomes for Stage Three:

The vertical axis on the diagram below represents the range of possible outcomes for Stage Three – Healthy Assertiveness (top) to Passiveness and Aggressiveness (bottom). The horizontal continuum represents the range of possible negative outcomes from frequently Externalizer to frequently Internalizer. Put an "X" anywhere on the diagram that fits with your position in your most intimate present day relationships (most of the time).

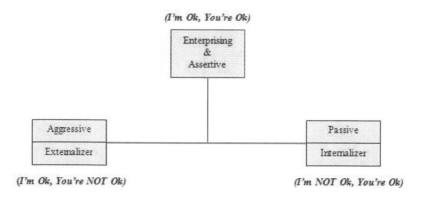

Figure 18: Stage Three Outcomes Continuum

Keep in mind that we can move around on this line depending upon the situation, circumstances, and especially what ego-state we are in (Angry Child, Vulnerable Child, Critical Parent, etc.). We are likely to stay in the Adult Ego-State at work or out in public.

In our private lives, especially if we are wounded, with loved ones and family members we cannot avoid being triggered into the Externalization of the Angry/Defiant Child and/or the Internalization of the Vulnerable/Needy Child ego-state. This is where and how the Drama Triangle, Figure-Eight, and other dysfunctional relationship patterns arise. (See THAW, Chapter 7.)

"Internalizers" or Codependents:

People who have disowned or cut themselves off (dissociated) from their Angry/Defiant Child ego-state tend to get caught up in the Internalizer role – such as those who were not allowed to express anger outwardly or perhaps a parent was abusive and a rage-a-holic so that it was dangerous to express your anger.

"Externalizers" or Counter-Dependents:

Those who have disowned or cut themselves off (dissociated) from their Vulnerable Child ego-state tend to gravitate toward the Externalizer position – such as those who were not allowed to have their feelings or families where vulnerable feelings were considered "weak."

Healthy, Positive Outcomes:

Those who had a predominantly positive outcome to this and all other stages are able to own and experience both their Angry/Defiant Child and their Vulnerable/Needy Child ego-states from an integrated position – i.e., because they have not been emotionally wounded, these two essential elements of self are simultaneously active and working together in harmony.

The Normal Function of the Vulnerable/Needy and Angry/Defiant Parts of Self:

A healthy Angry/Defiant Part provides access to just enough personal power to establish a sense of separateness while a healthy Vulnerable/Needy part helps let the walls down enough to really connect with others (only those who are safe and also able to connect in healthy ways). It is NOT having the ego-states (i.e., parts of self) that are the problem – it is the level of original pain that each of the parts carry that causes the reactivity.

Assertiveness, initiative, flexibility in thinking (vs. rigid "black or white" thinking), and judgment/criticism of self and/or others are the themes during this stage.

The extent to which we have a positive outcome directly influences our abilities to speak-up for ourselves, protect our rights, and respect the rights of others. If we have a negative outcome to this stage we will recycle through the negative emotional themes (abandonment, shame, and contempt) and recreate the experiences of this time in our development until we "get it right" – which is the goal of this section of the program.

Journal Assignment:

Think about how this diagram and issues fit with you and those closest to you. Which outcomes did each of your parents demonstrate most often? How about your past and present relationships? Which outcomes did you and your partners tend to demonstrate? Do you see any patterns or other interesting observations? Note your thoughts and observations in your journal.

[Audio Alert] Listen to Audio Program 31a – Relationship Timelines

Journal Assignment: Write about issues regarding your ability to be assertive, stand up for yourself, and share with others that you encountered on your Adult relationship timeline.

[Audio Alert] Listen to Audio Program 31b – Relationship Timelines

Journal Assignment: Write about issues regarding your ability to be assertive, stand up for yourself, and share with others that you encountered on your childhood relationship timeline.

3:4 Detecting Your Inner Critic:

[Audio Alert] Listen to Audio Program 32a – Inner Critic

This exercise helps to give a form to the critical voice or voices you hear inside your head, so that your Ideal Adult/Parent ego-state can communicate with, challenge or confront the negativity. The critical voice for the Pre-Schooler Self may ridicule you for being selfish, shame you when someone pushes you around, and convinces you that you have no right to speak up for yourself. When externalizing, it may be a voice that suggests that you ignore other people's rights, demand what you want "or else!" and disregard their needs and feelings.

The part of us that carries these shaming messages from the past is our Critical Parent ego-state. We all need this part of us that can take a critical position in order to anticipate obstacles and help us avoid needless problems – but we don't need the shaming, the discounting, and the abusive tones and messages that came from those other sources. Since the Pre-Schooler-Self borders on barely-verbal, these "voices" may be more like a feeling than an actual voice at the time the child internalized the messages. As an adult, these feelings gathered in early childhood can get translated into "audio tapes."

Whether turned inward or outward, these inner voices can be very poisonous or toxic, and can take on many shapes and forms. Its messages are usually very clear, and can be very damaging to your Children within as well as relationships with others. When working with these critical voices, get support from Higher Power and Protector if needed. Most of your Inner Children will have a specific voice that haunts them from which they will need to be protected.

As you answer the following questions you may want to imagine yourself surrounded by a protective, spiritual light from your Higher Power ... don't be surprised if your Child Self answers differently than you the adult.

1. What critical statements to make about yourself?

2. What criticism do you most often make of others?

3. What words do you most often use when you blame yourself for something that goes wrong? What words do you most often use to blame others?

4. What negative statements do you make to yourself about your body and your sexuality?

5.   Where have you heard those statements before? Whose voice is this? Is it the voice of a parent? A relative? A teacher? A clergy member? Classmate? Coach?

6.   Are these statements that you have heard from society or through the media? Is this voice imagined or real?

7.   Imagine that you, as the Inner Adult, speak to this voice. Ask this voice what it wants. What is its positive intention? Is it trying to protect, teach, warn you? Is it trying to protect, teach, warn them?

8.   Using your least dominant hand, let your Inner Child draw a picture of this critical voice. Know that this picture represents shame, criticism, over responsibility, and rigidity carried from childhood.

When you have finished the picture, go back to the original critical statements in items 1 through 6 above and rewrite them in your journal. Then, next to each critical statement, write a positive affirmation. Notice your self-talk and formulate your affirmation as a response; i.e., if the self-talk uses first-person, then form the affirmation as a response in second-person. (See Examples.)

[Audio Alert] Listen to Audio Program 32b – Inner Critic 2

Examples:

Critical Statement: *If I speak up for myself he/she may leave me.*
Positive Affirmation: *When you speak up you strengthen the relationship because others will respect you more.*

Critical Statement: *They're so selfish!*
Positive Affirmation: *Others have a right and responsibility to take care of their needs too.*

NOTE:

Remember to have your Ideal Adult/Parent or your Higher Power interact with this Inner Critic whenever it appears. Have them to use these affirmations whenever you hear these wounding words. Reassure your Inner Child that the critical voice will no longer go unchallenged.

3:5 Stage Three: Issues and Symptoms

It's time to consolidate; review your answers from the Self-Assessment Questionnaire, Audio Programs, your observations about the Outcomes Diagram and journal entries for this stage of development. Now, complete the following Stage Three Inner Child Profile below.

It is important to take your time to complete this exercise as thoroughly as possible. Listen to the audio programs as many times as you find helpful or if you get stuck. Don't worry if you cannot find the root cause (i.e., original circumstances), but it is a big bonus if you do. You are likely to uncover even more information in later exercises that will help fill in the blanks. When that happens, just come back here and add anything else that comes up. Here is an example of the Issues and a format to write it out in your journal. Outline as many issues as you can come up with. You cannot over-do this work, but you can under-do it.

- **Identified Issue:** (Problematic behavior)
  I am very critical about the emphasis people put on the way they dress and the amount of money they have.
- **The Root Cause:** (Original Circumstances)
  My mother divorced my father when I was four. She said she couldn't stand the way he took care of himself. She shamed him for not have a high-paying job. Dad

felt he was not good enough for Mom. He always felt ashamed of himself after that.

- **Evidence in Present Day:** (How I treat myself) I am highly critical of my attire and never feel comfortable or secure in the way I am dressed.

[Audio Alert] Listen to Audio Program 33a – Reclaim this Child

Your Pre-Schooler Self may carry pain, but it also carries courage, creativity, confidence, and inquisitiveness. You may now have a better awareness of these. In the exercises, you have done so far, what have you learned about your Pre-Schooler self and about how you continue to carry these traits? Write about any thoughts or feelings this question, and audio 33a has provoked.

[Audio Alert] Listen to Audio Program 33b – Adult Meets Child

These meetings with your Inner Children can be emotional; sometimes it's like meeting a stranger, other times it's like meeting an old friend. Record your thoughts, feelings, and reactions to this audio below. End the experience by asking your Pre-Schooler-Self to help you find a photograph or a picture from a magazine that looks like him or her. Paste or tape this picture into your journal so you can look at it and began to ask more in-depth questions and then write about how this picture makes you feel.

3:6 Communication and Daily Dialogue

The exercise will help the Adult-Self separate further from your Children within by helping you determine their likes and their dislikes. It also gives your Child-Self a chance to ask you questions. In this way, the Adult and Child begin to develop a healing and healthy relationship. Here you go inside and imagine having a conversation with your Inner Pre-Schooler. Record the conversation in your journal. This can become a "daily dialogue" if you choose.

If you do not get verbal answers from your Child within, try to interpret body language, feelings, sounds, or other sensations that you can intuit. Some people feel they communicate best with this part of themselves using a form of imaginary telepathy. If that works for you, use it. As you work with the older Children within, their ability to communicate will mature.

To begin your dialogue, write each question in your journal using your most dominant hand. Use your least dominant hand to record your Inner Children's responses. Use the name for the Child that you chose in the previous visualization exercise.

1. Does your Pre-Schooler have a favorite bedtime story? A favorite toy? A favorite play place? Ask the Child to show them to you.

2. What activity does your Pre-Schooler most enjoy?

3. Ask your Inner Pre-Schooler to tell you about his or her fear of being blamed and criticized or of doing or saying something wrong. These feelings may have been experienced back in the Child's day or the Child may experience these fears in relation to your life here-and-now.

4. Ask the Child to tell you what his/her life is like at that time. Find out if this Child feels overly responsible? Why?

5. What does this Child need the most from you? Ask the Child how it was treated by its caretakers, and if it is afraid that you will do the same.

6. How does this Child feel about you? Does it feel abandoned or ignored by you? Why? Does the Pre-Schooler understand what it means to be reclaimed by you? If not, explain that it means you will attempt to

maintain a balance between the opposing feelings within you. You will protect this Child from the criticism and judgments of others.

7. Does your Pre-Schooler within feel comfortable that you won't shame, blame or compare it with others?

8. Is there anything the Pre-Schooler wants to know about you?

Learn to use this journal exercise daily by tuning into the feelings you have throughout the day and realizing that it may be one of your Inner Children signaling you that they need your attention. Remember the format for "feelings as signals from your Inner Child" to know when the Child needs to talk with you.

3:7 Developing a Protector

Each Inner Child may want to have its own Protector, sometimes more than one. Start by letting your Child within first create the one that it needs the most. This Protector is the character you bring in to provide special care that the Adult Self is unable to provide.

Creating a Protector is a way to ensure that your Inner Child will never be alone. It's as if this Protector is assigned to your Inner Child and will always be there to care, even when your Adult Self is occupied in your day-to-day affairs. There are no guidelines for creating this Protector, let your Inner Children be your guide.

Journal Exercise:
1. Ask the Child within to tell you about the person or character for which it feels the most trust. If your Child can select anyone in the world, real or imagined, to always be there, who would the Child choose? (It can be Superman, an angel, Mother Teresa, or your Higher

Power. It can also be a relative, movie star, or a childhood friend's parent.)

2. Ask your Inner Child to draw a picture that represents this Protector. Have the Child use crayons or colored pencils and use the least dominant hand to draw the picture.

3. Assure your Inner Child that this Protector will be available any time the Child needs that Protector.

Keep this picture in your journal and keep it stored in your imagination, too. Always be ready to call in this Protector for support in your work with your Pre-Schooler Child. This character will care for, protect, and entertain your Child. It is this image that will help meet the emotional needs of your Child and heal the gaps left from the Child.

Complete this exercise by making a partnership between this Protector and the Adult-Self. Call in your Higher Power as well, if this seems appropriate, because these three make up the team that will heal the Children within. Record any thoughts, feelings, or other reactions to this exercise in your journal.

3:8 Grieving your Losses

This exercise will take you step-by-step through the grieving process so that you may let go of the blocked emotions from this stage of your development. You have gathered a lot of information from the previous exercises. Don't worry if you don't feel you have many answers to the following questions in this stage. Trust your instinct, let the answers come to you intuitively, and do the best you can.

Some steps of this process are done by you as the Adult, and some are done by you as the Inner Child. Remember to use your least dominant hand when responding from the Child and your dominant hand when responding from the Adult. This will help you more easily switch back and forth between these two parts of yourself.

Journal Exercises:

You will need your journal, drawing materials, and separate sheets of paper. *Do these exercises* on the *loose sheets of paper* – not in your journal. Everyone grieves in his own way. If any section of these exercises does not seem right for you, just discard or change that section and complete the ones that do seem to fit.

1. In your mind's-eye, see your Preschooler Child in front of you. Ask that part of you to consider times/events in the past when you felt panic, hurt, sadness, shame, or fear related to your ability to be assertive, take the initiative, be flexible in thinking (vs. rigid "black or white" thinking), and judgment/criticism of self and/or others. List these events one-by-one and then prioritize them from least painful to most painful. For our purposes here, don't worry about describing the events or experiences in detail ... just give them a name such as "that time in the kitchen with so-and-so." If the experience is too painful, just use one or two words to describe it for now such as "kitchen."

2. Now ask your Inner Child to draw a picture representing the feelings he or she has carried over the years (artistic talent not required). Have the Child draw one picture for each of the events or experiences you just listed above from least painful to most painful. Then, reflect on any other times in your life when you felt panic, hurt, or fear related to your ability to be assertive, take the initiative, be flexible in thinking (vs. rigid "black or white" thinking), and judgment/criticism of self and/or others ....draw a picture for any of these times you feel would be appropriate (no more than ten examples).

3. Now, as your Adult-Self, think back to the times you've tried to control these situations in your life so you wouldn't have to feel these feelings. Then list the survival skills your Little Professor devised to try to manipulate, bargain, or control in an attempt to get this Child's needs for safety, nurturing, or trust met at those times (e.g., hostility, aggressiveness, victim or persecutor stance, angry outbursts, distancing or pursuing, addictions, etc.).

4. Now, as your Adult-Self, write a letter explaining to your Pre-Schooler self that it was not his/her fault that their needs were unmet and, in your own words, tell the Child that the problems in the family were not caused by him/her either. Furthermore, describe to your Child the way it should have been and anything you know about why it was not that way. Be supportive, encouraging, and give the child permission to break the "Don't Talk, Don't Feel, Don't Trust" rules. Let this part of you know it is okay to have your feelings now because you are here to protect and allow that.

5. Now, help your Pre-Schooler write a letter to your parents expressing any anger, sadness, grief and other feelings that your Child has held over the years. As you finish the letter, let any feelings surface and come out as you comfort your Inner Child. (You might want to use a teddy bear and rocking chair combined with the sanctuary or other safe place of your own choosing to facilitate this experience.)

6. When you feel ready to continue, as the healthy Adult you, write a letter to your Pre-Schooler-Self stating how you feel about the care he or she received. Tell your Child within what you're willing to provide for him or her from this time forward. Imagine your Adult-Self reading this letter to your Inner Child somewhere, one-on-one in the sanctuary. Again, as you complete this,

imagine that you comfort your Child-Self in whatever way seems best to you.

7.   Conclude this grieving process by closing your eyes and surround yourself and your Inner Child with spiritual light from your Higher Power. In the next step, all the pain that has been express will be released in all the wounds that have been opened will be healed. Take a cleansing breath and bring your focus back to the room and open your eyes.

3:9 Releasing Blocked Emotions

This exercise lets your Inner Child release the pain in two ways: emotionally, and spiritually. For the process of emotional release, you will need the following items: your journal, all your drawings and writings from the previous step, a copy of the picture of your Inner Child, and a campfire (outside) or fireplace (inside). If inside, scented candles, background music (CD) and a comfortable, safe space where you won't be interrupted are also suggested.

Again, if any section of these exercises does not seem right for you, just discard or modify that section and complete the ones that do seem to fit:

Emotional Release ...

1.   Set up your space, light your candles if you choose, and put on your music. Now, take all the drawings, writings, and letters that you prepared in the previous steps and decide which ones you feel you need to release in the fire. Also, have your picture of this Child nearby.

2.   Imagine the light within your body begins to grow and expand until it surrounds you and fills up the entire room/area. Now, in your mind's-eye, bring in your Child-Self ... hold him or her safely in your arms, or comfortably settle your Pre-Schooler Child somewhere

in the room/area. You may want to use a teddy bear to symbolize the younger Children within.

3. Focus on the feelings you will be releasing. Mentally review the work you and your Child have done, the issues you have discovered, and the healing you have experienced so far. Now, silently ask your Child if he or she is ready to let go of its pain.

4. When the two of you are ready, take one of the drawings, letters, or pieces of writing and symbolically release it by dropping it into the fire. Imagine the emotions represented on that piece of paper are released into the flame and carried away by the smoke. Release your Inner Child's drawing that represents the panic and fear, your list of bargaining behaviors, the anger, despair and any other letters or written work you feel a need to release. Burn one piece of paper at a time, so you're able to focus on the contents of that page.

3:10 Release and Reimprinting this Stage

[Audio Alert] Listen to Audio Program 34a – Spiritual Release

Now record this experience in your journal. This Child has much joy and adventure to offer once the trust is there that you will meet his or her needs. Know that if the pain of this younger self gets triggered that you will be able to separate from the pain by letting the Child remain safely in the Sanctuary while the Adult you attends to the triggering situation.

Your fears of setting boundaries and your caution about taking risks may never completely disappear. In fact, it would not even be desirable to have them gone. It is important to be able to determine when it is safe and appropriate to trust as well as when it is not. Just know that, by completing this work the wounds of abandonment have been treated and a healing process initiated. You will get better and better, every day in every way!

[Audio Alert] Listen to Audio Program 34b – Parental Timeline Reimprinting

Listen to the audio at least two times or more. Really allow the ideas and images to become vivid and know that you are giving yourself more options by doing so. Write about your experience of the audio in your journal.

[Bonus Audio] Return to Audio #1: Majestic Meadow

As an extra benefit you may complete this work with your Inner Child by returning to Majestic Meadow and the garden of your thoughts. Ask your Inner Pre-Schooler how it would like to contribute to this garden now. It may choose certain plants or flowers to symbolically represent a new perspective, healing, and/or the gifts it can now bring to your experiences. Imagine that the two of you make these contributions together so that this Inner Child will be represented in the garden of your growth.

Stage Four – Industry vs. Inferiority
School-Aged (6-12 years old)

When a child is old enough, they must go off to school. It's another world for them, and now they have a full day of challenges to face. Furthermore, they are no longer the center of attention as they begin comparing themselves to each other. If children have had successful outcomes in the preceding stages, they are likely to be prepared to make the transition smoothly.

However, because the outcomes in each previous stage set the foundation for the next stages of social development, some children start out with challenges other kids do not have to face. Along with the multitude of rapid-fire changes involved in attending school, these kids also must contend with negative outcomes such as shame, fear, and guilt, which complicate these tasks even further.

Many parents tell their kids that they "are in school to learn something – not to socialize." This could not be further from the truth. Learning to fit in with their peers can give them the confidence and sense of competence to excel academically as well. It is therefore, very important to help them acquire good social skills – and as with anything else, that takes practice.

Kids who are bright academically but less than talented socially may become loners, shy and inhibited. They can develop a sense of inferiority despite their excellent academic achievements. Kids who are socially gifted can, likewise, develop a sense of inferiority if they are less able to succeed in the classroom. They may find ways to compensate for their intellectual shortcomings through sports or music.

In many cases, kids who have a negative outcome in this stage are likely to strengthen their leanings toward being an Internalizer or Externalizer. The Internalizer wears their sense of inferiority like a badge, while the Externalizer covers theirs up behind a mask of grandiosity.

Internalizers tend to seek others out to follow and take care of; seeking their approval, attention, protection, and validation from someone they perceive as stronger than themselves. Because they are frequently drawn to the opposite direction, they attach themselves to Externalizers and end up being made fun of, pregnant, abused, and/or dropping out – unless they have the ability to make it academically despite their social difficulties.

Externalizers at this stage of development are the rebels, delinquents, bullies, and "hard-cases" who get all the negative attention. They have over-compensated for their sense of inferiority through a reaction formation. Their outward grandiosity is a smokescreen to cover up their inward feelings of fear and inadequacy. Other kids escape into video games or anything else they can master and feel the enthusiasm of accomplishment – even if it's dangerous, such as extreme sports, fighting, or drugs to name a few.

4:1 Stage Four Self-Assessment
Unmet needs in each child development stage can be observed in present-day symptoms. For each of the following statements assign a rank between 10 (high) and 0 (not at all).

____ I feel unaccepted by most of my peers.

____ I feel judged by most people my age or by those in my profession.

____ I feel I have little in common with people my own age, or those in my profession.

____ I feel excluded from the activities of others.

____ I do not belong to organizations because I feel self-conscious.

____When I go to social gatherings, I feel out of place.

____ I am more comfortable being alone than with a group of friends.

___The groups I have participated in feel closed, and I have not felt a part of the "clique."

___ I avoid certain professional positions because I would have to talk in front of others.

___ I get physical symptoms of anxiety whenever I'm faced with speaking in front of a group.

___ I am unable to speak spontaneously in front of others. I must plan exactly what I want to say before it is my turn.

___Even if I feel strongly about a subject, I will not speak in public because I get too tongue-tied.

___When I speak in public, I'm not aware of anyone else in the room. I do not feel nervous, but I do seem to be disconnected from myself and others.

___ I describe myself as a procrastinator and feel lazy when it comes to getting things done.

___ I worry about going into business for myself; for fear that I do not have the self-discipline to succeed.

___ I have sabotaged by professional advancement because of my inability to meet deadlines.

___ I feel clumsy participating in any sport.

___ I have intense fear of making a mistake

___ I feel excessively competitive

___ I feel deficient in many things that most people consider basic life skills

___ I must win at any cost, or I'm terrible

___ I feel ugly and inferior; social shame, I go into a nice restaurant and feel like I don't belong there

___ In team sports, I fear being chosen last.

___ I refuse to participate in a sports activity in which I feel self-conscious.

___ I have become a "human-doing"; achievement is the only thing that matters

4:2 Journaling Exercise:
What do your answers reveal to you about your comfort level with competence and confidence? If you scored six or above on any item, those are the issues of your Pre-Schooler Self you will want to address.

1. Do you worry about being accepted by your peers? Can you think of a time when this was the case? Describe what it feels like to review this situation now that you have more information on this stage of your development.

2. Have there been times when you're worried about standing out? If so, when?

3. Have there been times when you were in the "in group" and have been aware of someone who was excluded? How did you feel? What, if anything, did you do?

4. Make a list of similarities and differences you see in yourself and three of your closest friends. How you feel about this?

5. List your professional goals. Do you feel satisfied with your achievements? If not, why?

6. List the emotional, social, and physical characteristics of your parents. Next, make a list of their professional and financial achievements. How do you compare to them, what does this say about your need to remain loyal, or your capacity to surpass your parents?

7. Whose opinion do you value more than your own? About which subjects? Why do you not trust your own opinions in this area? How do you feel about this? How does this affect your belief in yourself and your abilities?

8. Think of a situation where your inability to complete something jeopardized your career or a relationship. Describe the situation and comment on it now.

9. When you participate in a social event, do you feel energized or drained?

10. Now, explore and combine all the data that you obtained from the developmental questionnaire and these journal questions to make a list of issues your Inner School-Aged Self carries. Some examples are:

    a. Feeling self-conscious in social gatherings
    b. Difficulty, or inability, to complete something you've started
    c. Not being able to attain professional goals
    d. Keeping yourself in debt so you never achieve financial stability
    e. Fear of public speaking

4:3 Diagram of Possible Outcomes for Stage Four:
The vertical axis on the diagram below represents the range of possible outcomes for Stage Three – Healthy Competence (top) to Inferiority and Grandiosity (bottom). The horizontal continuum represents the range of possible negative outcomes from frequently Externalizer to frequently Internalizer. Put an "X" anywhere on the diagram that fits with your position in your most intimate present day relationships (most of the time).

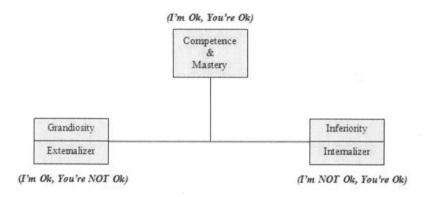

Figure 19: Stage Four Outcomes Continuum

Keep in mind that we can move around on this line depending upon the situation, circumstances, and especially what ego-state we are in (Angry Child, Vulnerable Child, Critical Parent, etc.). We are likely to stay in the Adult Ego-State at work or out in public.

In our private lives, especially if we are wounded, with loved ones and family members we cannot avoid being triggered into the Externalization of the Angry/Defiant Child and/or the Internalization of the Vulnerable/Needy Child ego-state. This is where and how the Drama Triangle, Figure-Eight, and other dysfunctional relationship patterns arise. (See THAW, Chapter 7.)

"Internalizers" or Codependents:

People who have disowned or cut themselves off (dissociated) from their Angry/Defiant Child ego-state tend to get caught up in the Internalizer role – such as those who were not allowed to express anger outwardly or perhaps a parent was abusive and a rage-a-holic so that it was dangerous to express your anger.

"Externalizers" or Counter-Dependents:

Those who have disowned or cut themselves off (dissociated) from their Vulnerable Child ego-state tend to gravitate toward the Externalizer position – such as those who were not allowed to have their feelings or families where vulnerable feelings were considered "weak."

Healthy, Positive Outcomes:

Those who had a predominantly positive outcome to this and all other stages are able to own and experience both their Angry/Defiant Child and their Vulnerable/Needy Child ego-states from an integrated position; i.e., because they have not been emotionally wounded, these two essential elements of self are simultaneously active and working together in harmony.

The Normal Function of the Vulnerable/Needy and Angry/Defiant Parts of Self:

A healthy Angry/Defiant Part provides access to just enough personal power to establish a sense of separateness while a healthy Vulnerable/Needy part helps let the walls down enough to really connect with others (only those who are safe and also able to connect in healthy ways). It is NOT having the ego-states (i.e., parts of self) that are the problem – it is the level of original pain that each of the parts carry that causes the reactivity.

Competence, mastery, and fitting in with peers at the themes for this stage.

The extent to which we have a positive outcome directly influences our abilities to feel confident, share our thoughts and feelings, and/or respect the thoughts and feelings of others. If we have a negative outcome to this stage we will recycle through the negative emotional themes (abandonment, shame, and contempt) and recreate the experiences of this time in our development until we "get it right" – which is the goal of this section of the program.

Journal Assignment:

Think about how this diagram and issues fit with you and those closest to you. Which outcomes did each of your parents demonstrate most often? How about your past and present relationships? Which outcomes did you and your partners tend to demonstrate? Do you see any patterns or other interesting observations? Note your thoughts and observations in your journal.

[Audio Alert] Listen to Audio Program 41a – Relationship Timelines

Journal Assignment: Write about issues regarding your ability to be feel confident, express yourself in a crowd, and feel "good enough" compared to others that you encountered on your Adult relationship timeline.

[Audio Alert] Listen to Audio Program 41b – Relationship Timelines

Journal Assignment: Write about issues regarding your ability to feel confident, express your thoughts and feelings, and feel "good enough" that you encountered on your childhood relationship timeline.

4:4 Detecting Your Inner Critic:

[Audio Alert] Listen to Audio Program 42a – Inner Critic

This exercise helps to give a form to the critical voice or voices you hear inside your head, so that your Ideal Adult/Parent ego-state can communicate with, challenge or confront the negativity. The critical voice between 6 and 12 is the voice that carries the haunting statements you heard at home and at school. This voice will tell you that you cannot succeed, that you will make a fool out of yourself, and that you should not even try. This voice will terrorize you when you have to appear in public, tell you that you'll never fit in, or that you look too fat, too ugly, or too thin.

The part of us that carries these shaming messages from the past is our Critical Parent ego-state. We all need this part of us that can take a critical position in order to anticipate obstacles and help us avoid needless problems – but we don't need the shaming, the discounting, and the abusive tones and messages that came from those other sources. As an adult, these feelings gathered in early childhood can get translated into "audio tapes."

Whether turned inward or outward, these inner voices can be very poisonous or toxic, and can take on many shapes and forms. Its messages are usually very clear, and can be very damaging to your children within as well as relationships with others. When working with these critical voices, get support from Higher Power and Protector if needed. Most of your Inner Children will have a specific voice that haunts them from which they will need to be protected.

As you answer the following questions you may want to imagine yourself surrounded by a protective, spiritual light from your Higher Power ... don't be surprised if your Child Self answers differently than you the Adult.

1. What critical statements to make about yourself when you have to appear in public or be around a crowd of strangers?

2. What critical statements do you make to yourself about your ability to succeed, or finish what you have started?

3.   What critical statements do you make to yourself when you could do something new or compete physically?

4.   What critical statements do you make to yourself when you begin to succeed or move ahead?

5.   Where have you heard those statements before? Whose voice is this? Is it the voice of a parent? A relative? A teacher? A clergy member? Classmate? Coach?

6.   Imagine that you, as the Inner Adult, speak to this voice. Ask this voice what it wants. What is its positive intention? Is it trying to protect, teach, warn you? Is it trying to protect, teach, warn them?

7.   Using your least dominant hand, let your Inner Child draw a picture of this critical voice. Know that this picture represents fear, terror, and judgments created by the critic within.

When you have finished the picture, go back to the original critical statements in items 1 through 6 above and rewrite them in your journal. Then, next to each critical statement, write a positive affirmation. Notice your self-talk and formulate your affirmation as a response; i.e., if the self-talk uses first-person, then form the affirmation as a response in second-person. (See Examples.)

[Audio Alert] Listen to Audio Program 32b – Inner Critic 2

Examples:

Critical Statement: *If I tell him/her what I really think he/she may get mad and leave me.*

Positive Affirmation: *When you share you true thoughts and feelings you strengthen the relationship because you are creating an authentic relationship.*

Critical Statement: *I'm so stupid!*
Positive Affirmation: *It's normal to make mistakes, even silly blunders once in a while.*

NOTE:

Remember to have your Ideal Adult/Parent or your Higher Power interact with this Inner Critic whenever it appears. Have them to use these affirmations whenever you hear these wounding words. Reassure your Inner Child that the critical voice will no longer go unchallenged.

4:5 Stage Four: Issues and Symptoms

It's time to consolidate. Review your answers from the Self-Assessment Questionnaire, Audio Programs, your observations about the Outcomes Diagram and journal entries for this stage of development. Now, complete the following Stage Four Inner Child Profile below.

It is important to take your time to complete this exercise as thoroughly as possible. Listen to the audio programs as many times as you find helpful or if you get stuck. Don't worry if you cannot find the root cause (i.e., original circumstances), but it is a big bonus if you do. You are likely to uncover even more information in later exercises that will help fill in the blanks. When that happens, just come back here and add anything else that comes up. Here is an example of the Issues and a format to write it out in your journal. Outline as many issues as you can come up with. You cannot over-do this work, but you can under-do it.

- **Identified Issue:** (Problematic behavior)
  I am very critical about the things that I say and the mistakes that I make.

- **The Root Cause:** (Original Circumstances)
  My mother was always pointing out the flaws in everybody and she frequently gossiped about the inferiority of others.
- **Evidence in Present Day:** (How I treat myself)
  I am driven by a need to be perfect. If I do ninety-nine things perfectly but I mess up on one thing, I cannot stop beating myself up for the mistake.

[Audio Alert] Listen to Audio Program 43a – Reclaim this Child

Your School-Aged Self may carry pain, but it also carries ability to learn, desire to be part of the group, determination, and persistence. You may now have a better awareness of these. In the exercises, you have done so far, what have you learned about your School-Aged Self and about how you continue to carry these traits? Write about any thoughts or feelings this question, and audio 33a has provoked.

[Audio Alert] Listen to Audio Program 43b – Adult Meets Child

These meetings with your Inner Children can be emotional; sometimes it's like meeting a stranger, other times it's like meeting an old friend. Record your thoughts, feelings, and reactions to this audio below. End the experience by asking your school-aged self to help you find a photograph or a picture from a magazine that looks like him or her. Paste or tape this picture into your journal so you can look at it and began to ask more in-depth questions and then write about how this picture makes you feel.

4:6 Communication and Daily Dialogue

The exercise will help the Adult-Self separate further from your Children within by helping you determine their likes and their dislikes. It also gives your Child Self a chance to ask you questions. In this way, the Adult and Child begin to develop a healing and healthy relationship. Here you go inside and imagine having a conversation with your Inner School-Aged Self. Record the conversation in your journal. This can become a "daily dialogue" if you choose.

If you do not get verbal answers from your Child within, try to interpret body language, feelings, sounds, or other sensations that you can intuit. Some people feel they communicate best with this part of themselves using a form of imaginary telepathy. If that works for you, use it. As you work with the older Children within, their ability to communicate will mature.

To begin your dialogue, write each question in your journal using your most dominant hand. Use your least dominant hand to record your Inner Children's responses. Use the name for the Child that you chose in the previous visualization exercise.

1. Does your School-Aged-Self have a favorite game? A favorite toy? Favorite play places? Ask the Child to show them to you.

2. What activity or school subject does your School-Aged Child most enjoy?

3. Ask your School-Aged-Self to tell you about his or her fear of being blamed and criticized or of doing or saying something wrong. These feelings may have been experienced back in the Child's day or the Child may experience these fears in relation to your life here-and-now.

4. Does this Child have an imaginary friend? If so, who is it? Find out if this Child feels overly responsible? Why?

5. What does this Child need the most from you? Ask the Child how it was treated by its caretakers, and if it is afraid that you will do the same. How does this Child like its brothers or sisters? Do they get along?

6. How does this Child feel about you? Does it feel abandoned or ignored by you? Why? Does the Child understand what it means to be reclaimed by you? If not, explain that it means you will attempt to maintain a balance between the opposing feelings within you. You will protect this Child from the criticism and judgments of others.

7. Does your Inner School-Aged Child feel comfortable that you won't shame, blame or compare it with others?

8. Is there anything the Pre-Schooler wants to know about you? Have this child tell you what its life has been like; including any pain, losses, or accidents experienced. What was it like to be at school?

9. What joys does this Child want to offer you and what prevents this from happening?

Learn to use this journal exercise daily by tuning into the feelings you have throughout the day and realizing that it may be one of your Inner Children signaling you that they need your attention. Remember the format for "feelings as signals from your Inner Child" to know when the Child needs to talk with you.

4:7 Developing a Protector

Each Inner Child may want to have its own Protector, sometimes more than one. Start by letting your Child within first create the one that it needs the most. This Protector is the character you bring in to provide special care that the Adult Self is unable to provide.

Creating a Protector is a way to ensure that your Inner Child will never be alone. It's as if this Protector is assigned to your Inner Child and will always be there to care, even when your Adult Self is occupied in your day-to-day affairs. There are no guidelines for creating this Protector, let your Inner Children be your guide.

Journal Exercise:

4. Ask the School-Aged Child to tell you about the person or character for which it feels the most trust. If your Child can select anyone in the world, real or imagined, to always be there, who would choose? (It can be Superman, an angel, Mother Teresa, or your Higher Power. It can also be a relative, movie star, or a childhood friend's parent.)

5. Ask your Inner Child to draw a picture that represents this Protector. Have the Child use crayons or colored pencils and use the least dominant hand to draw the picture.

6. Assure your Inner Child that this Protector will be available any time the Child needs that Protector.

Keep this picture in your journal and keep it stored in your imagination, too. Always be ready to call in this Protector for support in your work with your School-Aged Child. This character will care for, protect, and entertain your Child. It is this image that will help meet the emotional needs of your Child and heal the gaps left from the Child.

Complete this exercise by making a partnership between this Protector and the Adult-Self. Call in your Higher Power as well, if this seems appropriate, because these three are the team that will heal the Children within. Record any thoughts, feelings, or other reactions to this exercise in your journal.

4:8 Grieving your Losses

This exercise will take you step-by-step through the grieving process so that you may let go of the blocked emotions from this stage of your development. You have gathered a lot of information from the previous exercises.

Don't worry if you don't feel you have many answers to the following questions in this stage. Trust your instinct, let the answers come to you intuitively, and do the best you can.

Some steps of this process are done by you as the Adult, and some are done by you as the Inner Child. Remember to use your least dominant hand when responding from the Child and your dominant hand when responding from the Adult. This will help you more easily switch back and forth between these two parts of yourself.

Journal Exercises:

You will need your journal, drawing materials, and separate sheets of paper. *Do these exercises* on the *loose sheets of paper* – not in your journal. Everyone grieves in his own way. If any section of these exercises does not seem right for you, just discard or change that section and complete the ones that do seem to fit.

1. In your mind's-eye, see your School-Aged Child in front of you. Ask that part of you to consider times/events in the past when you felt panic, hurt, sadness, shame, or fear related to "fitting in" socially, personal success, competence and mastery. List these events one by one and then prioritize them from least painful to most painful. For our purposes here, don't worry about describing the events or experiences in detail … just give them a name such as "that time in the kitchen with so-and-so." If the experience is too painful, just use one or two words to describe it for now such as "kitchen."

2. Now ask your Inner Child to draw a picture representing the feelings he or she has carried over the years (artistic talent not required). Have the Child draw one picture for each of the events or experiences you just listed above from least painful to most painful.

Then, reflect on any other times in your life when you felt panic, hurt, or fear related to "fitting in" socially, personal abilities, lack of a sense of competence and confidence ... draw a picture for any of these times you feel would be appropriate (no more than ten examples).

3.　Now, as your Adult Self, think back to the times you've tried to control these situations in your life so you wouldn't have to feel these feelings. Then list the survival skills your Little Professor devised to try to manipulate, bargain, or control in an attempt to get this Child's needs for acceptance, competence, and "fitting-in" met at those times (e.g., people-pleasing, approval-seeking, care-taking, rescuing others, taking the martyr role, having "justified" anger, distancing or pursuing, addictions, etc.).

4.　Now, as your Adult Self, write a letter explaining to your School-Aged Self that it was not his/her fault that his needs were unmet and, in your own words, tell the Child that the problems in the family were not caused by him/her either. Furthermore, describe to your Child the way it should have been and anything you know about why it was not that way. Be supportive, encouraging, and give the Child permission to break the "Don't Talk, Don't Feel, Don't Trust" rules. Let this part of you know it is okay to have your feelings now because you are here to protect and allow that.

5.　Now, help your School-Aged Child write a letter to your parents expressing any anger, sadness, grief and other feelings that your Child has held over the years. As you finish the letter, let any feelings surface and come out as you comfort your Inner Child. (You might want to use a teddy bear and rocking chair combined with the sanctuary or other safe place of your own choosing to facilitate this experience.)

6.   When you feel ready to continue, as the healthy Adult you, write a letter to your School-Aged-Self stating how you feel about the care he or she received. Tell your Child within what you're willing to provide for him or her from this time forward. Imagine your Adult-Self reading this letter to your Inner Child somewhere, one-on-one in the sanctuary. Again, as you complete this, imagine that you comfort your Child-Self in whatever way seems best to you.

7.   Conclude this grieving process by closing your eyes and surround yourself and your Inner Child with spiritual light from your Higher Power. In the next step, all the pain that has been express will be released in all the wounds that have been opened will be healed. Take a cleansing breath and bring your focus back to the room and open your eyes.

4:9 Releasing Blocked Emotions
This exercise lets your Inner Child release the pain in two ways: emotionally, and spiritually. For the process of emotional release, you will need the following items: your journal, all your drawings and writings from the previous step, a copy of the picture of your Inner Child, and a campfire (outside) or fireplace (inside). If inside, scented candles, background music (CD) and a comfortable, safe space where you won't be interrupted are also suggested.

Again, if any section of these exercises does not seem right for you, just discard or modify that section and complete the ones that do seem to fit:

Emotional Release...
1.   Set up your space, light your candles if you choose, and put on your music. Now, take all the drawings, writings, and letters that you prepared in the previous steps and decide which ones you feel you need to

release in the fire. Also, have your picture of this Child nearby.

2.   Imagine the light within your body begins to grow and expand until it surrounds you and fills up the entire room/area. Now, in your mind's-eye, bring in your Child-Self ... hold him or her safely in your arms, or comfortably settle your School-Aged Child somewhere in the room/area. You may want to use a teddy bear to symbolize the younger Children within.

3.   Focus on the feelings you will be releasing. Mentally review the work you and your Child have done, the issues you have discovered, and the healing you have experienced so far. Now, silently ask your Child if he or she is ready to let go of the pain.

4.   When the two of you are ready, take one of the drawings, letters, or pieces of writing and symbolically release it by dropping it into the fire. Imagine the emotions represented on that piece of paper are released into the flame and carried away by the smoke. Release your Inner Child's drawing that represents the panic and fear, your list of bargaining behaviors, the anger, despair and any other letters or written work you feel a need to release. Burn one piece of paper at a time, so you're able to focus on the contents of that page.

4:10 Release and Reimprinting this Stage

[Audio Alert] Listen to Audio Program 44a – Spiritual Release

Now record this experience in your journal. This Child has much joy and adventure to offer once the trust is there that you will meet his or her needs. Know that if the pain of this younger self gets triggered that you will be able to separate from the pain by letting the Child remain safely in the

Sanctuary while the Adult you attends to the triggering situation.

Your fears of setting boundaries and your caution about taking risks may never completely disappear. In fact, it would not even be desirable to have them gone. It is important to be able to determine when it is safe and appropriate to trust as well as when it is not. Just know that, by completing this work the wounds of abandonment have been treated and a healing process initiated. You will get better and better, every day in every way!

[Audio Alert] Listen to Audio Program 44b – Parental Timeline Reimprinting

Listen to the audio at least two times or more. Really allow the ideas and images to become vivid and know that you are giving yourself more options by doing so. Write about your experience of the audio in your journal.

[Bonus Audio] Return to Audio #1: Majestic Meadow

As an extra benefit you may complete this work with your Inner Child by returning to Majestic Meadow and the garden of your thoughts. Ask your Inner School-Aged Self how it would like to contribute to this garden now. It may choose certain plants or flowers to symbolically represent a new perspective, healing, and/or the gifts it can now bring to your experiences. Imagine that the two of you make these contributions together so that this Inner Child will be represented in the garden of your growth.

Stage Five – Identity vs. Identity Diffusion
Early Adolescence (13-15 years old)
Late Adolescence (15-20 years old)

The "Terrible Twos" was the first appearance of the Angry/Defiant Child ego-state, but the official debut is the onset of adolescence. We have all known a 13 year-old with a chip on his or her shoulder – and it doesn't come off for several years. This is the beginning of a very tumultuous time for kids, which includes rapid-fire physical, emotional, social, and psychological changes.

The main task of adolescence is to answer the question "Who am I?" The answer to this question will determine many things in life, especially for teens who have been emotionally wounded in previous stages of development.

Remembering that the subconscious mind is our most faithful servant, we must be careful about what we store up in there. We must also remember that each stage of development prior to this sets the foundation upon which we build. Teenagers have a bigger challenge than others due to negative outcomes in prior stages – it's like starting off with a disability (often called low self-esteem).

Teens with low self-esteem may range from not engaging at all in these developmental urges – resulting in emotional arrest – all the way to the opposite extreme being overly-engaged to the point of becoming uncontrollable. The good news is that no matter how things went earlier in life, we are not destined to be stuck with those outcomes.

Since adolescents tend not to know who they are, they can get caught up in being what others want them to be in order to gain approval and acceptance. Alternatively, they may think that they can never become anything and give up trying to connect – becoming chronically depressed, or isolating, or getting into drugs and alcohol.

Loyalty is a major virtue picked up in this stage of development – loyalty to self, to others, and to our own values and beliefs. Teens with low self-esteem tend to be a bit too loyal to others who are not as good to them in return.

There are four stages of adolescent development within this stage of human development:

- **Separation** – This stage of adolescent development begins with puberty at about 12 to 13 years old. It can be like the "Terrible 13's" when new teenagers find that they have a mouth and an opinion to go with it. They can become restless, irritable, and discontent ... not to mention downright rude and obnoxious. This causes strife, pitting them against their parents, which is a subconscious maneuver that helps them begin pulling away initiating the second major emotional separation.

- **Individuation** - In this stage of adolescent development the teenager will "try on" different roles like they would a new outfit in order to find the one that best fits them. They may try out being an athlete one day, a musician the next, and a sophisticated intellectual the next day. They may experiment with alcohol or smoking to see how they fit with their emerging personality.

  Reputation and image among peers become of paramount importance during this time. Some kids take refuge in the stance that "I fit in all groups," freely moving from one group to another rather than making a commitment to one group in particular.

- **Rebellion** - With the new driver's license can come a new attitude ... it's like "I have arrived!" in adulthood. Smoking, drinking parties and other "grown-up" behaviors are now fair game. Privacy and space to be a teenager are now demanded – or all hell may (and sometimes does) break loose. Anti-authority, anti-social, anti-conformist attitudes help the teenager take mom and dad down off the pedestal, so they can begin to "break the apron strings" in preparation to leave the nest soon and become fully functioning, independent human beings.

In order to make a clean getaway, kids rebel in equal proportion to how strongly parents try to hold on to the old ways. In this stage, it's time to begin redefining the nature of the relationship away from parent-to-child toward parent-to-young-adult – a major adjustment and a time of grief for many parents.

- **Cooperation** - About 18-19 through 21-23 years old is the time when teens become young adults. They have usually left home and discovered that fighting the system doesn't help them get what they want. They learn to cooperate with their environment in order to reach their goals in life ... both short-term and long-term. They take out their body piercings, cover up their tattoos, change their hair back to one color BEFORE going to that job interview ... and revert back to their "normal" self during their off hours.

5:1 Stage Five Self-Assessment

Unmet needs in each child development stage can be observed in present-day symptoms. For each of the following statements assign a rank between 10 (high) and 0 (not at all).

___ I have difficulty going to social functions by myself because I feel so nervous.

___ I get tongue-tied if I run into an acquaintance unexpectedly.

___ If I go to party, I tend to stay pretty close to the person I came with. I feel too shy to talk to new people.

___ I am uncomfortable in public. I feel self-conscious, as if people are watching me.

___ I feel uncomfortable with my body; it's too fat, too thin, too short, too long, too different.

___ I am sexually inhibited.

___ I like the lights off when I'm having sex.

___ I feel uncomfortable when I'm around a person to whom I feel attracted.

___ I need a second opinion on the decisions I make.

___ If I am wearing an accessory I like and someone makes an unflattering comment, I take it off.

___ If I am in a group of people, I notice the one person who does not seem to like me.

___ I have a hard time trusting my own judgments, so I rely on those close to me to determine what is appropriate.

___ I smoke, do drugs, or drink alcohol excessively.

___When I receive news that is hard to handle, I behave in a way that later results in negative consequences.

___Whenever life gets tough, I bury myself in work.

___Whenever I am upset, sex is the only activity that settles me down. It doesn't matter with whom; I just know that I need that release.

___When I feel panic, I seek relief with alcohol, drugs, cigarettes, shopping, gambling, eating, etc.

___ I engage in destructive activity that has severe consequences on my finances, relationships or my health.

___If someone tries to order me around, I am unable to stand up for myself.

___ I have lost jobs because when my bosses asked me to do something I did not want to do, I reacted hastily or angrily.

___If I'm driving on the freeway and someone cuts me off, I catch up with the car and try to intimidate the driver by tailgating or yelling profanities.

___If I'm losing an argument, I storm out of the room and refuse to discuss the matter any further.

___If my boss asked me to do something that I do not want to do, I will agree but then forget or fail to complete the job.

___If the driver behind me flashes his lights indicating he wants me to move out of the fast lane, I ignore and slow down even more, so that the driver is forced to go around me.

___If my partner or spouse behaves the way I do not like, I will retaliate by spending money, not coming home, her secretly going out with someone else.

___ I am very concerned with what my partner/spouse wears in public.

___ I get angry at my partner or supervisor when confronted with the way I behave.

___ I agree with the political beliefs of those close to me.

___ Even if I do not like the styles, I buy clothes that the magazines say are the most fashionable because I want to fit in and be like everyone else.

___ I feel if you saw me in a crowd, you would not notice me because there's nothing about me that stands out.

5:2 Journaling Exercise:

What do your answers reveal to you about your comfort level with competence and confidence? If you scored six or above on any item, those are the issues of your Teenaged-Self you will want to address.

The information about your social, physical, and sexual awkwardness should be self-explanatory. If you do not remember specific situations, memories may become clearer as you work on this healing process.

The information you get about your dependency on approval from others can be little more complicated. It is important to feel you can ask someone what they think. We all need feedback. Dependency is when you completely lose sight of what you wanted to do because you value another's opinion so greatly. Dependency may vary for different areas and relationships in your life.

If you are in early recovery from an addiction, your Addict Self (Rebellious Teen) has been running your life to such a degree that you may not have access to a responsible part of you (Parent ego-state) that you can trust. 12-Step programs, proven to be the most effective treatment for addiction, are built on the concept of powerlessness and a need to trust in a power greater than you. One must have a long period of abstinence from addictive behavior before trusting in oneself again. If the questions on addictive behavior indicate you may have a problem; now is the time to reach out for help.

Early Teenager (13 to 15 years old)

1. With which aspects of your sexuality do you feel comfortable?

2. With which aspects of your sexuality do you feel uncomfortable?

3.   How do you reach decisions about lovemaking? It's this comfortable for you? If not, why not?

4.   When did you attend your last social function? Who did you go with? How did you feel?

5.   Do use any drugs or alcohol? Do you feel you have a problem with chemical use? Do you have to "use" something before you go on a date, attend a social event, or have sex?

6.   In what areas of your life do you feel the most confident trusting your own judgment? Why?

7.   Have you ever thought you may be an incest survivor? Have you ever discussed this with anyone? Do you feel it is necessary to explore this possibility now? If so, what do you plan to do?

8.   As you think back over the ages of 12 to 15, reflect on the strengths that you may have acquired.

9.   Now, explore and combine all the data that you obtained from the developmental questionnaire and these journal questions to make a list of **issues your early teen carries**. Some examples are:

   • Being sexually shy or inhibited
   • Having an inappropriate need for others' approval
   • Using substances or destructive behavior to cope with discomfort in life
   • Feeling socially inadequate
   • Feeling overly conscious about physical appearance

Late Teenager (15 to 20 years old)

1. In what areas of your life do you feel rebellious?

2. How do you rebel? Does it work? List times when your rebellion seemed to get in your sense of self and then times when it seemed to sabotage your efforts instead?

3. Have you ever lost a job, home, friend or a lover because of your rebellious nature?

4. Do you start diets, exercise, or health programs and then rebel and stop?

5. Do you feel angry or rebellious about other people's behavior? If so, list some of these situations.

6. Write any other thoughts or feelings about rebellion.

7. What is unique about you? Do you feel comfortable with those qualities? Do others appreciate those qualities or do they try to challenge them?

8. What would it take for you to encourage your individuality? (You may see this in the way you dress, or activities in which to participate.) If you allow yourself to express your uniqueness, you will find little need to rebel.

9. In what areas of your life do you feel you compromise your beliefs or identity? Is there anyone in your life on whom you depend for money or for emotional support? Who pays rent, your bills, your car payment, your entertainment? How do you feel about that?

10. Now, explore and combine all the data that you obtained from the developmental questionnaire and these journal questions to make a list of issues your Inner Adolescent carries. Some examples are:

- Been caught in an active or passive state of rebellion
- Inability to stand up for yourself
- Being very controlling and critical of another's behavior
- Over-involvement in a lover or spouses life because that person is a reflection of you
- Been so afraid to stand out that you never discover what your own tastes are

5:3 Diagram of Possible Outcomes for Stage Five:

The vertical axis on the diagram below represents the range of possible outcomes for Stage Three – Healthy Sense of Self (top) to More-than-Human and Less-then-Human (bottom). The horizontal continuum represents the range of possible negative outcomes from frequently Externalizer to frequently Internalizer. Put an "X" anywhere on the diagram that fits with your position in your most intimate present day relationships (most of the time).

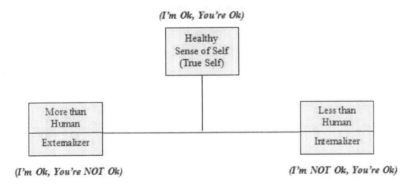

Figure 20: Stage Five Outcomes Continuum

Keep in mind that we can move around on this line depending upon the situation, circumstances, and especially what ego-state we are in (Angry Child, Vulnerable Child, Critical Parent, etc.) We are likely to stay in the Adult Ego-State at work or out in public.

In our private lives, especially if we are wounded, with loved ones and family members we cannot avoid being triggered into the Externalization of the Angry/Defiant Child and/or the Internalization of the Vulnerable/Needy Child ego-state. This is where and how the Drama Triangle, Figure-Eight, and other dysfunctional relationship patterns arise. (See THAW, Chapter 7.)

"Internalizers" or Codependents:

People who have disowned or cut themselves off (dissociated) from their Angry/Defiant Child ego-state tend to get caught up in the Internalizer role – such as those who were not allowed to express anger outwardly or perhaps a parent was abusive and a rage-a-holic so that it was dangerous to express your anger.

"Externalizers" or Counter-Dependents:

Those who have disowned or cut themselves off (dissociated) from their Vulnerable Child ego-state tend to gravitate toward the Externalizer position – such as those who were not allowed to have their feelings or families where vulnerable feelings were considered "weak."

Healthy, Positive Outcomes:

Those who had a predominantly positive outcome to this and all other stages are able to own and experience both their Angry/Defiant Child and their Vulnerable/Needy Child ego-states from an integrated position – i.e., because they have not been emotionally wounded, these two essential elements of self are simultaneously active and working together in harmony.

The Normal Function of the Vulnerable/Needy and Angry/Defiant Parts of Self:

A healthy Angry/Defiant Part provides access to just enough personal power to establish a sense of separateness while a healthy Vulnerable/Needy part helps let the walls down enough to really connect with others (only those who are safe and also able to connect in healthy ways). It is NOT having the ego-states (i.e., parts of self) that are the problem – it is the level of original pain that each of the parts carry that causes the reactivity.

The ability to make choices, develop friendships, experiment with various roles in search of self, and discover and explore sexuality, resolve conflict, and break the ties of childhood are the themes in this stage.

The extent to which we have a positive outcome directly influences sense of competence, social skills, and sense of belonging. If we have a negative outcome to this stage we will recycle through the negative emotional themes (abandonment, shame, and contempt) and recreate the experiences of this time in our development until we "get it right" – which is the goal of this section of the program.

Journal Assignment:

Think about how this diagram and issues fit with you and those closest to you. Which outcomes did each of your parents demonstrate most often? How about your past and present relationships? Which outcomes did you and your partners tend to demonstrate? Do you see any patterns or other interesting observations? Note your thoughts and observations in your journal.

[Audio Alert] Listen to Audio Program 51a – Relationship Timelines

Journal Assignment: Write about issues regarding your ability to make good choices, maintain loyalty, deal with emotions, resolve conflict, and experiencing a healthy love life (sexually and emotionally) that you encountered on your adult relationship timeline.

[Audio Alert] Listen to Audio Program 51b – Relationship Timelines

Journal Assignment: Write about issues regarding your parents' abilities make good choices, maintain loyalty, resolve conflict, deal with emotions, and demonstrate healthy acceptance of sexuality that you encountered on your childhood relationship timeline.

5:4 Detecting Your Inner Critic:

[Audio Alert] Listen to Audio Program 52a – Inner Critic

This exercise helps to give a form to the critical voice or voices you hear inside your head, so that your Ideal Adult/Parent ego-state can communicate with, challenge or confront the negativity. The critical voice for the teenage years is the voice that will criticize you for not being yourself. It will tell you that you are a chicken and afraid to stand up for what you believe in. This voice carries all the critical statements about your social skills, attractiveness, ability to fit in, athletic abilities, and your uniqueness as a person. It is usually the voice(s) of all the adults and authority figures who were in your life at this time.

The part of us that carries these shaming messages from the past is our Critical Parent ego-state. We all need this part of us that can take a critical position in order to anticipate obstacles and help us avoid needless problems – but we don't need the shaming, the discounting, and the abusive tones and messages that came from those other sources.

Whether turned inward or outward, these inner voices can be very poisonous or toxic, and can take on many shapes and forms. Its messages are usually very clear, and can be very damaging to your children within as well as relationships with others. When working with these critical voices, get support from Higher Power and Protector if needed. Most of your Inner Children will have a specific voice that haunts them from which they will need to be protected.

As you answer the following questions you may want to imagine yourself surrounded by a protective, spiritual light from your Higher Power ... don't be surprised if your Child Self answers differently than you the Adult.

1.   What critical statements do you make to yourself about your struggle to be you?

2.   What critical statements do you make to yourself about your ability to stand up for yourself?

3.   What critical statements do you make to yourself when you feel your identity has been violated and that you either have overreacted or not reacted at all?

4.   What critical statements do you make about being unique and different?

5.   Where have you heard those statements before? Whose voice is this? Is it the voice of a parent? A relative? A teacher? A clergy member? Classmate? Coach?

6.   What critical statements do you make about your experiences with sex and sexuality?

7.   Are these statements that you have heard from society or through the media? Is this voice imagined or real?

8.   Imagine that you, as the Inner Adult, speak to this voice. Ask this voice what it wants. What is its positive intention? Is it trying to protect, teach, warn you?

9.   Let your Adolescent Self to draw or locate a picture of this critical voice. Know that this picture represents the judgments you make of yourself about being you.

When you have finished the picture, go back to the original critical statements in items 1 through 6 above and rewrite them in your journal. Then, next to each critical statement, write a positive affirmation. Notice your self-talk and formulate your affirmation as a response; i.e., if the self-talk uses first-person, then form the affirmation as a response in second-person. (See Examples.)

[Audio Alert] Listen to Audio Program 32b – Inner Critic 2

Examples:

Critical Statement: *If I tell them what I think they may laugh at me.*
Positive Affirmation: *When you share you true thoughts and stand behind them strengthens the respect others give you.*

Critical Statement: *I'm so stupid!*
Positive Affirmation: *It's normal to make mistakes, even silly blunders once in a while.*

NOTE:
Remember to have your Ideal Adult/Parent or your Higher Power interact with this Inner Critic whenever it appears. Have them to use these affirmations whenever you hear these wounding words. Reassure your Inner Child that the critical voice will no longer go unchallenged.

5:5 Stage Five: Issues and Symptoms

It's time to consolidate. Review your answers from the Self-Assessment Questionnaire, Audio Programs, your observations about the Outcomes Diagram and journal entries for this stage of development. Now, complete the following Stage Five Inner Child Profile below.

It is important to take your time to complete this exercise as thoroughly as possible. Listen to the audio programs as many times as you find helpful or if you get stuck. Don't worry if you cannot find the root cause (i.e., original circumstances), but it is a big bonus if you do. You are likely to uncover even more information in later exercises that will help fill in the blanks. When that happens, just come back here and add anything else that comes up. Here is an example of the Issues and a format to write it out in your journal. Outline as many issues as you can come up with. You cannot over-do this work, but you can under-do it.

- **Identified Issue:** (Problematic behavior)
  I am terribly uncomfortable in new situations. I would rather be alone than to confront the uneasiness I feel in strange surroundings.
- **The Root Cause:** (Original Circumstances)
  My family moved around a lot and I had to leave my friends many times. I never felt like I belonged anywhere.
- **Evidence in Present Day:** (How I treat myself)
  I become preoccupied with my appearance whenever I am going to someplace new. Sometimes it takes me hours to get ready and still I never get comfortable with how I look. I feel like I won't fit in no matter what.

[Audio Alert] Listen to Audio Program 53a – Reclaim this Child

Your Teenage Self may carry pain, but underneath it also carries your uniqueness, hopes and dreams, ambition, desire to contribute, and self-acceptance. You may now have a better awareness of these. In the exercises, you have done so far, what have you learned about your Teenage Self and about how you continue to carry these traits? Write any thoughts or feelings related to this exercise in your journal.

[Audio Alert] Listen to Audio Program 53b – Adult Meets Child

These meetings with your Inner Children can be emotional; sometimes it's like meeting a stranger, sometimes it's like meeting an old friend. Record your responses to this exercise in your journal. End the experience by asking your Teenage Self to help you find a photograph or a picture from a magazine that looks like him or her. Paste or tape this picture into your journal so you can look at it and began to ask more in-depth questions and then write about how this picture makes you feel.

5:6 Communication and Daily Dialogue

The exercise will help the Adult-Self separate further from your Children within by helping you determine their likes and their dislikes. It also gives your Child Self a chance to ask you questions. In this way, the Adult and Child begin to develop a healing and healthy relationship. Here you go inside and imagine having a conversation with your Inner Teenage Self. Record the conversation in your journal. This can become a "daily dialogue" if you choose.

If you do not get verbal answers from your Child within, try to interpret body language, feelings, sounds, or other sensations that you can intuit. Some people feel they communicate best with this part of themselves using a form of imaginary telepathy. If that works for you, use it.

To begin your dialogue, write each question in your journal using your most dominant hand. Use your least dominant hand to record your Inner Teenager's responses. Use the name for the child that you chose in the previous visualization exercise.

Early Teenager:

1. Does your Teenager-Self have a favorite game? A favorite hobby? Favorite activities? Ask the Child to show them to you.

2. What is your Teen's favorite song, favorite pastime, and favorite subject in school?

3. How does your Teen get along with family members and friends? Does your Teen date, have a boyfriend or girlfriend, work or just hang out?

4. Does your Inner Teen understand the feeling of awkwardness? Is your Teen willing to tell you about his or her uneasiness?

5. Have this younger you tell you what its life has been like, including any pain, losses, or accidents experienced. What was it like to be you at this time in your life?

6. How does this Child feel about you? Does it feel abandoned or ignored by you? Why? Does the Child understand what it means to be reclaimed by you? If not, explain that it means you will attempt to maintain a balance between the opposing feelings within you. You will protect this Child from the criticism and judgments of others.

7. What does this Teen need the most from you? Ask the Child how it was treated by its peers, and if it is afraid that you will do the same.

8. Is there anything this younger you wants to know about the Adult you?

9. What joys does this Inner Teenager want to offer you and what prevents this from happening?

Late Teenager:

1. Does your older Teenager-Self have a favorite game? A favorite hobby? Favorite activities? Ask the Child to show them to you.

2. What is this Teen's favorite band, favorite pastime, sport, and favorite subject in school?

3. How does your Teen get along with family members and friends? Does this Teen date, have a boyfriend or girlfriend, work, or just hang out?

4. Ask your Adolescent within to tell you about any time he/she felt violated, rejected or abused, and about the struggle experienced with trying to discover who he or she really is.

5. Have this younger you tell you what life has been like; including any pain, losses, or accidents experienced. What was it like to be you at this time in your life?

6. How does this Child feel about you? Does it feel abandoned or ignored by you? Why? Does the Child understand what it means to be reclaimed by you? If not, explain that it means you will attempt to maintain a balance between the opposing feelings within you. You will protect this Child from the criticism and judgments of others.

7. What does this Teen need the most from you? Ask the Child how it was treated by its peers, and if it is afraid that you will do the same.

8. Is there anything this younger you wants to know about the adult you?

9. What joys does this Inner Teenager want to offer you and what prevents this from happening?

Learn to use this journal exercise daily by tuning into the feelings you have throughout the day and realizing that it may be one of your Inner Children signaling you that they need your attention. Remember the format for "feelings as signals from your Inner Child" to know when the Child needs to talk with you.

5:7 Developing a Protector

Each Inner Child may want to have its own Protector, sometimes more than one. Start by letting your Child within first create the one that it needs the most. This Protector is the character you bring in to provide special care that the Adult Self is unable to provide.

Creating a Protector is a way to ensure that your Inner Child will never be alone. It's as if this Protector is assigned to your Inner Child and will always be there to care, even when your Adult Self is occupied in your day-to-day affairs. There are no guidelines for creating this Protector, let your Inner Children be your guide.

Journal Exercise:

1. Ask the School-Aged Child to tell you about the person or character for which it feels the most trust. If your Child can select anyone in the world, real or imagined, to always be there, who would choose? (It can be Superman, an angel, Mother Teresa, or your Higher Power. It can also be a relative, movie star, or a childhood friend's parent.)

2. Ask your Inner Child to draw a picture that represents this Protector. Have the Child use crayons or colored pencils and use the least dominant hand to draw the picture.

3. Assure your Inner Child that this Protector will be available any time the Child needs that Protector.

Keep this picture in your journal and keep it stored in your imagination, too. Always be ready to call in this Protector for support in your work with your Teenaged Child. This character will care for, protect, and entertain your Child. It is this image that will help meet the emotional needs of your Child and heal the gaps left from the Child.

Complete this exercise by making a partnership between this Protector and the Adult-Self. Call in your Higher Power as well, if this seems appropriate, because these three make up the team that will heal the Children within. Record any thoughts, feelings, or other reactions to this exercise in your journal.

4:8 Grieving your Losses

This exercise will take you step by step through the grieving process so that you may let go of the blocked emotions from this stage of your development. You have gathered a lot of information from the previous exercises. Don't worry if you don't feel you have many answers to the following questions in this stage. Trust your instinct, let the answers come to you intuitively, and do the best you can.

Some steps of this process are done by you as the Adult, and some are done by you as the Inner Child. Remember to use your least dominant hand when responding from the Child and your dominant hand when responding from the Adult. This will help you more easily switch back and forth between these two parts of yourself.

Journal Exercises:

You will need your journal, drawing materials, and separate sheets of paper. *Do these exercises* on the *loose sheets of paper* – not in your journal. Everyone grieves in his or her own way. If any section of these exercises does not seem right for you, just discard or change that section and complete the ones that do seem to fit.

1. In your mind's-eye, see your Teenaged Child in front of you. Ask that part of you to consider times/events in the past when you felt panic, hurt, sadness, shame, or fear related to social life and status, self-image, personal choices, getting along with others, and conflicts with authority. List these events one by one and then prioritize them from least painful to most painful. For our purposes here, don't worry about describing the events or experiences in detail ... just give them a name such as "that time in the kitchen with so-and-so." If the experience is too painful, just use one or two words to describe it for now such as "kitchen."

2. Now ask your Inner Child to draw a picture representing the feelings he or she has carried over the years (artistic talent not required). Have the Child draw one picture for each of the events or experiences you just listed above from least painful to most painful. Then, reflect on any other times in your life when you felt panic, hurt, or fear about social life and status, self-image, personal choices, getting along with others, and conflicts with authority. Make a list of examples (no more than ten examples).

3. Now, as your Adult Self, think back to the times you've tried to control these situations in your life so you wouldn't have to feel these feelings. Then list the survival skills your Little Professor devised to try to manipulate, bargain, or control in an attempt to get this Child's needs for peer acceptance, competence, and "fitting-in" met at those times (e.g., people-pleasing, approval-seeking, care-taking, rescuing others, taking the martyr role, having "justified" anger, distancing or pursuing, addictions, etc.).

4. Now, as your Adult Self, write a letter explaining to your Teenaged Self that it was not his/her fault that those needs were unmet and, in your own words, tell the Child that the problems in the family, or in the past, were not caused by him/her either. Furthermore, describe to your Child the way it should have been and anything you know about why it was not that way. Be supportive, encouraging, and give the Child permission to break the "Don't Talk, Don't Feel, Don't Trust" rules. Let this part of you know it is okay to have your feelings now because you are here to protect and allow that.

5. Now, help your Teenager write a letter to your parents expressing any anger, sadness, grief and other feelings that your Child has held over the years. As you finish the letter, let any feelings surface and come out as you comfort your Inner Child. (You might want to use a teddy bear and rocking chair combined with the sanctuary or other safe place of your own choosing to facilitate this experience.)

6. When you feel ready to continue, as the healthy Adult you, write a letter to your Teenager-Self stating how you feel about the care he or she received. Tell your Child within what you're willing to provide for him or her from this time forward. Imagine your Adult-Self reading this letter to your Inner Child somewhere, one-on-one in the sanctuary. Again, as you complete this, imagine that you comfort your Child-Self in whatever way seems best to you.

7. Conclude this grieving process by closing your eyes and surround yourself and your Inner Child with spiritual light from your higher power. In the next step, all the pain that has been express will be released in all the wounds that have been opened will be healed. Take

a cleansing breath and bring your focus back to the room and open your eyes.

5:9 Releasing Blocked Emotions

This exercise lets your Inner Child release the pain in two ways: emotionally, and spiritually. For the process of emotional release, you will need the following items: your journal, all your drawings and writings from the previous step, a copy of the picture of your Inner Child, and a campfire (outside) or fireplace (inside). If inside, scented candles, background music (CD) and a comfortable, safe space where you won't be interrupted are also suggested.

Again, if any section of these exercises does not seem right for you, just discard or modify that section and complete the ones that do seem to fit:

Emotional Release...

1.   Set up your space, light your candles if you choose, and put on your music. Now, take all the drawings, writings, and letters that you prepared in the previous steps and decide which ones you feel you need to release in the fire. Also, have your picture of this Child nearby.

2.   Imagine the light within your body begins to grow and expand until it surrounds you and fills up the entire room/area. Now, in your mind's-eye, bring in your Child-Self ... hold him or her safely in your arms, or comfortably settle your Teenage Child somewhere in the room/area. You may want to use a teddy bear to symbolize the younger Children within.

3.   Focus on the feelings you will be releasing. Mentally review the work you and your Child have done, the issues you have discovered, and the healing you have experienced so far. Now, silently

ask your Child if he or she is ready to let go of her pain.

4.   When the two of you are ready, take one of the drawings, letters, or pieces of writing and symbolically release it by dropping it into the fire. Imagine the emotions represented on that piece of paper are released into the flame and carried away by the smoke. Release your Inner Teen's drawing that represents the panic and fear, your list of bargaining behaviors, the anger, despair and any other letters or written work you feel a need to release. Burn one piece of paper at a time, so you're able to focus on the contents of that page.

5:10 Release and Reimprinting this Stage

[Audio Alert] Listen to Audio Program 54a – Spiritual Release

Now record this experience in your journal. This Teen has much joy and adventure to offer once the trust is there that you will meet his or her needs. Know that if the pain of this younger self gets triggered that you will be able to separate from the pain by letting the Child remain safely in the Sanctuary while the Adult you attends to the triggering situation.

Your fears of not fitting in and of not fitting in may never completely disappear. In fact, it would not even be desirable to have them gone. It is important to be able to determine when it is safe and appropriate to trust as well as when it is not. Just know that, by completing this work, the wounds of abandonment have been treated and a healing process initiated. You will get better and better, every day in every way!

[Audio Alert] Listen to Audio Program 54b – Parental Timeline Reimprinting

Listen to the audio at least two times or more. Really allow the ideas and images to become vivid and know that you are giving yourself more options by doing so. Write about your experience of the audio in your journal.

[Bonus Audio] Return to Audio #1: Majestic Meadow

As an extra benefit you may complete this work with your Inner Teen by returning to Majestic Meadow and the garden of your thoughts. Ask your Inner Teenage Self how it would like to contribute to this garden now. It may choose certain plants or flowers to symbolically represent a new perspective, healing, and/or the gifts it can now bring to your experiences. Imagine that the two of you make these contributions together so that this Inner Adolescent will be represented in the garden of your growth.

Stage Six– Intimacy vs. Isolation (Self-Absorption)
Young Adulthood (20-30)

This stage of development involves our abilities to love and work with others. These abilities are directly affected through a consolidation of the outcomes of the previous child development stages:

- **Stage One** sets the tone for our ability to trust and feel safe – the ability to trust and feel safe helps us connect.

- **Stage Two** sets the tone for how well we can maintain a separate sense of self. Autonomy allows us to separate from mother.

- **Stage Three** sets the tone for how well we can explore new things and initiate intimate interactions.

- **Stage Four** sets the tone for our ability to feel confident and competent in life and in relationships.

- **Stage Five** sets the tone for how well we can maintain our identity and balance in our lives.

What is Intimacy?

The term intimacy is often viewed through the very narrow focus of sexual activity. This is a mistake – first of all, because strangers can have sex and never be even remotely intimate in the true sense of the word. Secondly, healthy sexual intimacy is a reward of having built an authentically intimate relationship.

Adding sexual intercourse to a relationship too soon can be like injecting it with poison; there are too many strings, expectations, and emotional baggage that come with this decision. If one or both partners are not at a place where these issues can be worked through and talked out all sorts of problems result – if there are not enough intimacy skills available to either person the new relationship cannot survive these problems.

True intimacy is free of psychological games such as the Figure-Eight and Drama Triangle. It occurs in those rare moments of human contact that arouse such feelings as desire, tenderness, empathy, vulnerability, affirmation and affection. Intimacy combines genuine giving and receiving with the candidness of "game-free" communication.

Authenticity is the core element of healthy intimacy. This is where I am able to share who I really am, and what I really think and feel with you and you are healthy enough to do, likewise.

What is Isolation?

Some level of isolation is the result when developmental outcomes have not been consistently positive in the previous child development stages. Levels of isolation may be viewed on a continuum between an extreme avoidance of closeness to a relentless pursuit of enmeshment. In both cases, the person becomes absorbed in his own needs.

Here we see impairment in the ability to maintain a sense of separateness and connectedness in the relationship. Externalizers tend to have a strong conscious fear of being trapped while Internalizers tend to experience a strong conscious fear of abandonment.

A fear of being trapped or suffocated in a relationship provokes a need to create distance as a way of maintaining a separate sense of self. There are many distancing maneuvers employed by the Externalizer's Critical Parent and Angry/Defiant Child Ego States – here are a few:

•Frequent Fighting
•Emotional Absence (Numbing or Withdrawal)
•Physical Absence
•Work-a-holism
•Other Addictions

•Belittling a Partner
•Other Emotional or Physical Abuse
•Having Affairs

A fear of being abandoned in a relationship provokes a need to pursue, chase, or cling to a partner (which feels like suffocating and actually triggers the need to distance in their partner). There are many methods of pursuit employed by the Internalizer's Critical Parent and Vulnerable Child Ego States:

•Frequent Fighting
•Emotional Flooding (frequent crying, or rage, or both)
•Neediness or Being "Clingy"
•Frequent Phone Calls
•Care-taking and people-pleasing
•Constant need for reassurance that they are loved
•Lack of boundaries – fear of saying "No"
•Secretly "Stalking" a Partner

Distance and Pursuit Games

Since the above relationship styles are polar opposites (polarities) they tend to attract each other. This relationship dynamic sets up a constant game of distance and pursuit, also known as "Cat & Mouse."

When the Distancer's conscious fear of being trapped gets triggered, he/she distances from their partner. The distancing behavior feels like abandonment, which triggers the pursuer's conscious fear of abandonment causing them to pursue ... which then triggers more distancing ... which triggers more pursuit.

However, when the pursuer gives up the pursuit and begins to pull back, it feels like distancing ... which triggers a subconscious fear of abandonment in the Distancer. In other words, the Distancer's Vulnerable/Needy Child ego-state gets triggered and brings with it the fear of abandonment causing a polarity reversal (role reversal) where the Distancer begins to pursue.

This eventually gets the Pursuer's (now turned Distancer) attention triggering their Vulnerable/Needy Child causing them to turn around and attempt to enmesh, re-triggering the fear of being trapped in their partner, the Distancer who begins to distance again.

Pursuers are usually the Internalizer in the relationship...

Internalizers are driven by their Vulnerable/Child ego state (the part that helps us connect). They tend to repress their Angry/Defiant Child (the part that helps us separate) which is why the fear of being trapped is subconscious. Distancers often choose Pursuers because they have a subconscious fear of abandonment and Pursuers can't leave the relationship.

Distancers are usually the Externalizers in the relationship...

Being driven by their Angry/Defiant Child ego state, they tend to repress their Vulnerable/Needy Child causing the fear of abandonment to remain hidden – until the pursuer begins to distance. When the Distancer's fear of being trapped is removed because their partner begins to back away, there's an abandonment reaction from their repressed Vulnerable/Needy Child causing them to pursue.

So, Distance and Pursuit games are the only way a wounded couple can regulate separateness and connectedness in their relationship – until they get help to heal the wounds of the past.

6:1 Stage Six Self-Assessment
Unmet needs in each child development stage can be observed in present-day symptoms. For each of the following statements assign a rank between 10 (high) and 0 (not at all).

____ I rely on others to pay my rent, utilities, and food.

____ I am irresponsible about paying monthly bills on time.

____ I do not take care of my laundry, prepare my meals, and clean or contribute to cleaning my home.

____When someone asked me to do something even though I agree, I do not follow through.

____When I get parking or speeding tickets, I do not pay them on time.

____ If I cannot keep an appointment, instead of calling to cancel, I just do not show up.

____ If I harm or damage something that does not belong to me, I remain quiet and hope the owner does not notice.

____ I feel dissatisfied with where I am in my professional growth.

____ I feel unmotivated to pursue the credentials I need for me to do what I want professionally.

____ I do not select jobs that fully reflect my professional capabilities.

____ I am not successful in my relationships with coworkers.

6:2 Journaling Exercise:

What do your answers reveal to you about your comfort level with who you are? If you scored six or above on any item, those are the issues of your Young Adult Self you will want to address.

Keep in mind that the issues of your Young Adult are involved with how well you have moved into the world. Use the following questions to ascertain how you feel about your place in the world. Determine your successes and the areas in which you need to focus.

1.   What are your personal needs and how well do you take care of them?

2.   Is there anyone else who prepares your meals or takes care of any of your basic needs? How do you feel about this?

3.   Is there anyone for whom you are responsible? If so, who? How do you feel about this?

4.   In what areas of your life do you feel you are responsible? And what areas do you feel you're irresponsible?

5.   Do you have a professional dream? If so, what is it? Are you pursuing it? If not, why not?

6.   What are your financial goals? Do you have the financial knowledge and skills you need to achieve them?

7.   What are your interpersonal needs? Do you get them met? With friends, family, a lover, or spouse?

8.   Are these needs getting met?

9.   What, if any, are your spiritual or religious beliefs? Do you practice them?

10. Reflect on the strengths you may have developed because of your life experiences.

11. Now, explore and combine all the data that you obtained from the developmental questionnaire and these journal questions to make a list of issues your Inner School-Aged Self carries.

Some examples are:

a. Feeling self-conscious in social gatherings
b. Difficulty, or inability, to complete something you've started
c. Not being able to attain professional goals
d. Keeping yourself in debt so you never achieve financial stability
e. Fear of public speaking

6:3 Diagram of Possible Outcomes for Stage Four:

The vertical axis on the diagram below represents the range of possible outcomes for Stage Three – Healthy Intimacy (top) to All-About-Me and All-About-You (bottom). The horizontal continuum represents the range of possible negative outcomes from frequently Externalizer to frequently Internalizer. Put an "X" anywhere on the diagram that fits with your position in your most intimate present day relationships (most of the time).

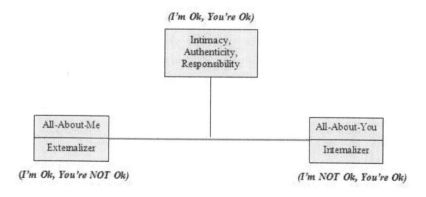

Figure 21: Stage Six Outcomes Continuum

Keep in mind that we can move around on this line depending upon the situation, circumstances, and especially what ego-state we are in (Angry Child, Vulnerable Child, Critical Parent, etc.) We are likely to stay in the Adult Ego-State at work or out in public.

In our private lives, especially if we are wounded, with loved ones and family members we cannot avoid being triggered into the Externalization of the Angry/Defiant Child and/or the Internalization of the Vulnerable/Needy Child ego-state. This is where and how the Drama Triangle, Figure-Eight, and other dysfunctional relationship patterns arise. (See THAW, Chapter 7.)

"Internalizers" or Codependents:

People who have disowned or cut themselves off (dissociated) from their Angry/Defiant Child ego-state tend to get caught up in the Internalizer role – such as those who were not allowed to express anger outwardly or perhaps a parent was abusive and a rage-a-holic so that it was dangerous to express your anger.

"Externalizers" or Counter-Dependents:

Those who have disowned or cut themselves off (dissociated) from their Vulnerable Child ego-state tend to gravitate toward the Externalizer position – such as those who were not allowed to have their feelings or families where vulnerable feelings were considered "weak."

Healthy, Positive Outcomes:

Those who had a predominantly positive outcome to this and all other stages are able to own and experience both their Angry/Defiant Child and their Vulnerable/Needy Child ego-states from an integrated position – i.e., because they have not been emotionally wounded, these two essential elements of self are simultaneously active and working together in harmony.

The Normal Function of the Vulnerable/Needy and Angry/Defiant Parts of Self:

A healthy Angry/Defiant Part provides access to just enough personal power to establish a sense of separateness while a healthy Vulnerable/Needy part helps let the walls down enough to really connect with others (only those who are safe and also able to connect in healthy ways). It is NOT having the ego-states (i.e., parts of self) that are the problem – it is the level of original pain that each of the parts carry that causes the reactivity.

The ability to maintain a sense of self, be authentic, emotionally present and engaged in the relationship, and be responsible for self are the themes of this stage.

The extent to which we have a positive outcome directly influences our abilities to feel confident, share our thoughts and feelings, and/or respect the thoughts and feelings of others. If we have a negative outcome to this stage we will recycle through the negative emotional themes (abandonment, shame, and contempt) and recreate the experiences of this time in our development until we "get it right" – which is the goal of this section of the program.

Journal Assignment:

Think about how this diagram and issues fit with you and those closest to you. Which outcomes did each of your parents demonstrate most often? How about your past and present relationships? Which outcomes did you and your partners tend to demonstrate? Do you see any patterns or other interesting observations? Note your thoughts and observations in your journal.

[Audio Alert] Listen to Audio Program 61a – Relationship Timelines

Journal Assignment: Write about issues regarding your abilities to be authentic, responsible, emotionally present, and how you handled conflict that you encountered on your adult relationships timeline.

[Audio Alert] Listen to Audio Program 61b – Relationship Timelines

Journal Assignment: Write about issues regarding your parent's ability to be confident, express their thoughts and feelings, and feel "good enough" that you encountered on your childhood relationship timeline. Did they give you permission and demonstrate the ability to feel confident, express your thoughts and feelings, and feel "good enough?"

6:4 Detecting Your Inner Critic:

[Audio Alert] Listen to Audio Program 62a – Inner Critic

This exercise helps to give a form to the critical voice or voices you hear inside your head, so that your Ideal Adult/Parent ego-state can communicate with, challenge or confront the negativity. The critical voice is the voice that carries the haunting statements you heard all your life to this point. This voice may tell you that you cannot succeed, that you will make a fool out of yourself, and that you should not even try. This voice will terrorize you, or others when directed outward (externalized) it may tell you that you'll never fit in, or that you look too fat, too ugly, or too thin.

The part of us that carries these shaming messages from the past is our Critical Parent ego-state. We all need this part of us that can take a critical position in order to anticipate obstacles and help us avoid needless problems – but we don't need the shaming, the discounting, and the abusive tones and messages that came from those other sources. As an adult, these feelings gathered in early childhood can get translated into "audio tapes."

Whether turned inward or outward, these inner voices can be very poisonous or toxic, and can take on many shapes and forms. Its messages are usually very clear, and can be very damaging to your Children within as well as relationships with others. When working with these critical voices, get support from Higher Power and Protector if needed. Most of your Inner Children will have a specific voice that haunts them from which they will need to be protected.

As you answer the following questions you may want to imagine yourself surrounded by a protective, spiritual light from your Higher Power ... don't be surprised if your Young Adult Self answers differently than you the Present Self:

1. What critical statements do you make to yourself about your ability to succeed?

2. What critical statements do you make to yourself about your ability to be responsible?

3. What critical statements do you make to yourself regarding your masculinity or femininity?

4. What critical statements do you make to yourself about the opposite sex?

5. What critical statements do you make to yourself about your professional achievements?

6. Where have you heard those statements before? Whose voice is this? Is it the voice of a parent? A relative? A teacher? A clergy member? A classmate? Coach? Are these statements that you have heard from society or through the media? Is this voice imagined or real?

7.   Imagine that you, as the Inner Adult, speak to this voice. Ask this voice what it wants. What is its positive intention? Is it trying to protect, teach, warn you?

8.   Create or find a picture of this critical voice. Know that this picture represents the feeling of fear and judgment created by the messages you received that said you would not, could not, should not succeed.

When you have finished the picture, go back to the original critical statements in items 1 through 6 above and rewrite them in your journal. Then, next to each critical statement, write a positive affirmation. Notice your self-talk and formulate your affirmation as a response; i.e., if the self-talk uses first-person, then form the affirmation as a response in second-person. (See Examples.)

[Audio Alert] Listen to Audio Program 32b – Inner Critic 2

Examples:

Critical Statement: *If I tell him/her what I really think he/she may get mad and leave me.*
Positive Affirmation: *When you share you true thoughts and feelings you strengthen the relationship because you are creating an authentic relationship.*

Critical Statement: *They are so stupid!*
Positive Affirmation: *It's normal to make mistakes, even silly blunders once in a while.*

NOTE:
   Remember to have your Ideal Adult/Parent or your Higher Power, interact with this Inner Critic whenever it appears. Have them to use these affirmations whenever you hear these wounding words. Reassure your Inner Child that the critical voice will no longer go unchallenged.

6:5 Stage Six: Issues and Symptoms

It's time to consolidate. Review your answers from the Self-Assessment Questionnaire, Audio Programs, your observations about the Outcomes Diagram and journal entries for this stage of development. Now, complete the following Stage Six Inner Young Adult Profile below.

It is important to take your time to complete this exercise as thoroughly as possible. Listen to the audio programs as many times as you find helpful or if you get stuck. Don't worry if you cannot find the root cause (i.e., original circumstances), but it is a big bonus if you do. You are likely to uncover even more information in later exercises that will help fill in the blanks. When that happens, just come back here and add anything else that comes up. Here is an example of the Issues and a format to write it out in your journal. Outline as many issues as you can come up with. You cannot over-do this work, but you can under-do it.

- **Identified Issue:** (Problematic behavior)
  I never seem able to pay my bills on time and my credit rating is such that I cannot even get a loan for a car.
- **The Root Cause:** (Original Circumstances)
  My parents were always short of money. There were seven kids and there never seemed to be enough of anything to go around. Most family crises centered on a lack of money.
- **Evidence in Present Day:** (How I treat myself)
  I do not pay my debt to my body on time. I don't go to the dentist or the doctor regularly. I am not responsible to my needs to eat or bathe on a consistent basis.

[Audio Alert] Listen to Audio Program 63a – Reclaim this Part

Your Young Adult Self may carry pain, but underneath it also carries all of your personal history; including past successes, lessons and understandings from past mistakes, and many inner resources – integrating all of this into the subconscious mind as wisdom. You may now have a better awareness of these. In the exercises you have done so far, what have you learned about your Teenage Self and about how you continue to carry these traits? Write any thoughts or feelings related to this exercise below.

[Audio Alert] Listen to Audio Program 63b – Adult Meets this Part

These meetings with your Inner Children can be emotional; sometimes it's like meeting a stranger, other times it's like meeting an old friend. Record your thoughts, feelings, and reactions to this audio below. End the experience by asking your Young Adult Self to help you find a photograph or a picture from a magazine that looks like him or her. Paste or tape this picture into your journal so you can look at it and began to ask more in-depth questions and then write about how this picture makes you feel.

6:6 Communication and Daily Dialogue

The exercise will help the Adult-Self separate further from your Children within by helping you determine their likes and their dislikes. It also gives your Young Adult Self a chance to ask you questions. In this way, the Adult and this part begin to develop a healing and healthy relationship. Here you go inside and imagine having a conversation with your Inner Young Adult Self. Record the conversation in your journal. This can become a "daily dialogue" if you choose.

If you do not get verbal answers from this part of you, try to interpret body language, feelings, sounds, or other sensations that you can intuit. Some people feel they communicate best with this part of themselves using a form of imaginary telepathy. If that works for you, use it. As you work with the older parts of self, their ability to communicate will mature.

To begin your dialogue, write each question in your journal using your most dominant hand. Use your least dominant hand to record your Inner Children's responses. Use the name for the Child that you chose in the previous visualization exercise.

1.   Ask your Young Adult what his or her or her favorite activity is.

2.   What plans does this Young Adult you have at this point in your life; college, a job, marriage, or following a dream?

3.   What are his or her dreams or aspirations? What would he or she most like to be?

4.   Ask your Younger adult within to tell you about the fears of not knowing how to succeed in the world. Is there any confusion about what role that Young Adult is supposed to play?

5.   What does this younger you need the most from the Adult you?

6.   How does this part of you feel about the Adult you? Does it feel abandoned or ignored by you? Why?

7.   Does the Young Adult understand what it means to be reclaimed by you? If not, explain that it means you will help your Young Adult learn what he or she needs to learn in order to succeed in the adult world. You'll take classes, read books, even higher nationals if need be, to ensure the needs of this Inner Child are met.

8.   Does your Young Adult need help preparing for college or have questions that only you can address?

9.   Is there anything your Young Adult wants to know about you? Are there any concerns he or she has about what you have done or are doing with your life?

Learn to use this journal exercise daily by tuning into the feelings you have throughout the day and realizing that it may be one of your Inner Children signaling for your attention. Remember the format for "feelings as signals from your inner parts" to know when the Child needs to talk with you.

6:7 Developing an Adviser

Your Young Adult will need inner role-models who can act as advisers for each of the adult tasks he or she has identified as issues, such as balancing your checkbook, enrolling in school, seeking other employment, buying a new car, how to invest your money, how to choose a mate, how to improve your social life, etc.

1. Focus on the issue for which you need the Adviser. Ask the Young Adult to tell you about a person or character for which it feels the most trust. If your Child can select anyone in the world, real or imagined, to always be there, who would choose?

2. If one cannot be identified, work together to create a Protector or Adviser. Make a list of all the characteristics an Adviser would need. Either draw or imagine in the image of the ideal adviser.

3. Create an Adviser for each issue.

Complete this exercise by making a partnership between this Adviser and the Adult-Self. Call in your Higher Power as well, if this seems appropriate, because these three make up the team that will heal the Children within. Record any thoughts, feelings, or other reactions to this exercise in your journal.

6:8 Grieving your Losses

This exercise will take you step-by-step through the grieving process so that you may let go of the blocked emotions from this stage of your development. You have gathered a lot of information from the previous exercises. Don't worry if you don't feel you have many answers to the following questions in this stage. Trust your instinct, let the answers come to you intuitively, and do the best you can.

Some steps of this process are done by you as the Present Adult, and some are done by you as the Younger Adult.

Journal Exercises:
You will need your journal, drawing materials, and separate sheets of paper. *Do these exercises* on the *loose sheets of paper* – not in your journal. Everyone grieves in his own way. If any section of these exercises does not seem right for you, just discard or change that section and complete the ones that do seem to fit.

1. In your mind's eye, see your Young Adult Self before you. Ask this part of you to consider times/events in the past when you felt anger, hurt, fear, sadness, or shame related to your abilities to be authentic, responsible, emotionally present, and how you handled conflict. List these events one by one and then prioritize them from least painful to most painful. For our purposes here, don't worry about describing the events or experiences in detail … just give them a name such as "that time in the kitchen with so-and-so." If the experience is too painful, just use one or two words to describe it for now such as "kitchen."

2. Now ask your Young Adult Self to draw or describe in written words a picture representing the feelings he or she has carried over the years (artistic talent not required). Have this part of you describe in writing or drawing each of the events or experiences you just listed above from least painful to most painful. Then, reflect on any other times in your life when you experienced anger, hurt, fear, sadness, or shame about

your abilities to be authentic, responsible, emotionally present, and how you handled conflict … draw or describe in words a picture for any of these times you feel would be appropriate (no more than ten examples).

3.   Now, as your Ideal Adult Self (True Self), think back to the times you've tried to control these situations in your life so you wouldn't have to feel these feelings. Then list the survival skills your Little Professor devised to try to manipulate, bargain, or control in an attempt to get this Child's needs for safety, nurturing, or trust met at those times (e.g., hostility, aggressiveness, persecutor stance, angry outbursts, distancing or pursuing, addictions, etc.).

4.   When you feel ready to continue, as the Adult Self (True Self) writes a letter to each of your Young Adult Selves stating how you feel about the mistakes and difficulties of that time. Tell your Young Adult Self what you're willing to provide for them from this time forward. Imagine your Adult-Self reading this letter to this part of you.

5.   Conclude this grieving process by closing your eyes and surrounding yourself and your Inner Child with spiritual light from your Higher Power. In the next step, all the pain that has been expressed will be released and all the wounds that have been opened will be healed. Take a cleansing breath and bring your focus back to the room and open your eyes.

6:9 Releasing Blocked Emotions

This exercise lets your Young Adult release the pain in two ways: emotionally and spiritually. For the process of emotional release, you will need the following items: your journal, all your drawings and writings from the previous steps, a copy of the picture of your Young Adult, and a campfire (outside) or fireplace (inside). If inside, scented candles, background music (CD) and a comfortable, safe space where you won't be interrupted are also suggested.

Again, if any section of these exercises does not seem right for you, just discard or modify that section and complete the ones that do seem to fit:

Emotional Release...

1. Set up your space, light your candles if you choose, and put on your music. Now, take all the drawings, writings, and letters that you prepared in the previous steps and decide which ones you feel you need to release in the fire. Also, have your picture of this Part nearby.

2. Imagine the light within your body begins to grow and expand until it surrounds you and fills up the entire room/area. Now, in your mind's-eye, bring in your Young-Adult-Self ... put your arm around that part of you, hold hands or find another way to connect in a supportive way.

3. Focus on the feelings you will be releasing. Mentally review the work you and your Younger Self have done, the issues you have discovered, and the healing you have experienced so far. Now, silently ask this Part if he or she is ready to let go of its pain.

4. When the two of you are ready, take one of the drawings, letters, or pieces of writing and symbolically release it by dropping it into the fire. Imagine the emotions represented on that piece of paper are released into the flame and carried away by the smoke. Release your Young-Adult-Self's drawing that represents the panic and fear, your list of bargaining behaviors, the anger, despair and any other letters or written work you feel a need to

release. Burn one piece of paper at a time, so you're able to focus on the contents of that page.

6:10 Release and Reimprinting this Stage

[Audio Alert] Listen to Audio Program 64a – Spiritual Release

Now record this experience in your journal. This Child has much joy and adventure to offer once the trust is there that you will meet his or her needs. Know that if the pain of this Younger Self gets triggered that you will be able to separate from the pain by letting the Younger you remain safely in the Sanctuary while the Present Adult you attends to the triggering situation.

Your fears of setting boundaries, being loved, and your caution about taking risks and trusting others may never completely disappear. In fact, it would not even be desirable to have them gone. It is important to be able to determine when it is safe and appropriate to trust as well as when it is not. Just know that, by completing this work the wounds of abandonment have been treated and a healing process initiated. You will get better and better, every day in every way!

[Audio Alert] Listen to Audio Program 64b – Parental Timeline Reimprinting

Listen to the audio at least two times or more. Really allow the ideas and images to become vivid and know that you are giving yourself more options by doing so. Write about your experience of the audio in your journal.

[Bonus Audio] Return to Audio #1: Majestic Meadow

As an extra benefit you may complete this work with your Young Adult by returning to Majestic Meadow and the garden of your thoughts. Ask your Young Adult Self how it would like to contribute to this garden now. It may choose certain plants or flowers to symbolically represent a new perspective, healing, and/or the gifts it can now bring to your experiences. Imagine that the two of you make these contributions together so that this younger you will be represented in the garden of your growth.

Sustaining Growth

Congratulations! You have completed *Thawing Childhood Abandonment Issues*. It may be worthwhile to write in your journal about the thoughts and feelings you have as you look back over the past weeks of work and all healing you have put in.

What to Expect Now

It is important to now that while you have just made huge strides in healing the wounds of abandonment, shame, and contempt, that you are likely to experience thoughts and feelings that are habitual remnants of the programming that has been in place all your life. Your recovery is not over, but the initial "emotional surgery" is done. You no longer have to "live life in reaction" to those old survival skills. Now is the time for long-term healing and growth to continue.

Recovery is a journey that gets better and better as you continue changing, growing and self-actualizing. It has been said many times that "if you keep doing what you are doing, you will keep getting what you are getting." That was true before you began this journey – you kept getting what you didn't like because you kept doing what you were programmed to do. It remains true now that you have completed your first trip through this program – so if you like what you have been getting, then keep doing what you are doing.

Intensity and repetition are two mechanisms that the brain uses to program (and re-program) itself. For that reason alone it would be a good thing to complete this program again whenever you feel like doing so. Another reason is if you feel "incomplete"… or perhaps you intuitively feel the need to do a specific stage again. You may begin right away, or in six months, or even a year later. Each time through is like peeling an onion until you get to the core. There is no way to know whether that will be in one trip or three. It is available now when and if you need it again.

Reminder – A Safe Container

One must create a "safe container" in recovery and going forward in life. This means having a support network of people who know what you are going through, such as a therapist, a support group such as Adult Children of Dysfunctional Families or Codependents Anonymous, a sponsor, safe, supportive friends, and/or safe, supportive family members.

There are many more resources available for free on my website at **www.Internet-of-the-Mind.com**. When you come by to visit the web site, check out the Oasis @ Serenity Café. The Oasis is a membership site that has tons of audios, eBooks, online versions of the Thawing the Iceberg Series, downloadable content, and programs, a forum and a social community of people healing these same issues.

Thanks for using the Thawing the Iceberg Series! Other Books and Materials in the series includes: *Thaw – Freedom from Frozen Feelings, Thawing Adult Child Syndrome,* and *Thawing Your Relationships.*

Appendix A
Suggested Readings and Resources

Don's Web sites:
www.Internet-of-the-Mind.com (Don's main web site)
www.Oasis-connections.com (aka, Oasis @ Serenity Café)
  The Oasis is Don's Membership site, loaded with resources and the Audios referred to in the "Audio Alerts" in this book.
www.Don-Carter.com
www.OasisforAuthors.com

Suggested Reading Materials:
Don Carter, (2010) Thaw – Freedom from Frozen Feeling-States
Don Carter, (2010) Thawing Adult/Child Syndrome
Don Carter, (2011) Thawing Your Relationships
John Bradshaw (2005) Healing the Shame that Binds You
John Bradshaw (1992) Homecoming: Reclaiming and Championing Your Inner Child
Charles L. Whitfield (1987) Healing the Child Within: Discovery and Recovery for Adult Children of Dysfunctional Families
Charles L. Whitfield (1990) A Gift to Myself: A Personal Workbook and Guide to "Healing the Child Within"
Charles L. Whitfield (1991) Co-Dependence - Healing the Human Condition
Pia Mellody, Andrea Wells Miller, and J. Keith Miller (1992) Facing Love Addiction: Giving Yourself the Power to Change the Way You Love
Pia Mellody, Andrea Wells Miller, and J. Keith Miller (1989) Facing Codependence: What It Is, Where It Comes from, How It Sabotages Our Lives
Pia Mellody and Lawrence S. Freundlich (2004) The Intimacy Factor: The Ground Rules for Overcoming the Obstacles to Truth, Respect, and Lasting Love
John J. Ratey (2002) A User's Guide to the Brain: Perception, Attention, and the Four Theaters of the Brain

Abraham Maslow (1968) Toward a Psychology of Being

Matthew Linn, Sheila Fabricant, and Dennis Linn (1988) Healing the Eight Stages of Life

Sharon Wegscheider-Cruse (1991) The Family Trap: No one escapes from a chemically dependent family

John Joseph Powell (1995) Why Am I Afraid to Tell You Who I Am? Insights into Personal Growth

Rick Warren (2002, 2007) The Purpose Driven Life

Craig Nakken (1996) The Addictive Personality: Understanding the Addictive Process and Compulsive Behavior

Melody Beattie (1992) Codependent No More: How to Stop Controlling Others and Start Caring for Yourself

Claude Steiner (1994) Scripts People Live: Transactional Analysis of Life Scripts

Eric Berne (1996) Games People Play: The Basic Handbook of Transactional Analysis

William Horton, Ph.D. (2008) Personal Correspondence: Email

Ronald A. Ruden; Marcia Byalick (1997) Craving Brain: The Biobalance Approach to Controlling Addiction

AAWS (2002) Alcoholics Anonymous: The Story of How Many Thousands of Men and Women Have Recovered from Alcoholism

Terence T. Gorski and Merlene Miller (1986) Staying Sober: A Guide for Relapse Prevention

Terence T. Gorski (1997) by Passages through Recovery: An Action Plan for Preventing Relapse

Made in the USA
Lexington, KY
20 September 2012